1985

**Ethics on a
Catholic University Campus**

Top photo:
Loyola's President,
Father Raymond Baumhart, S.J.,
opens the 1980
Loyola-Baumgarth Symposium.

Bottom photo:
Foreground:
Father Raymond Baumhart, S.J., and
Father Thomas McMahon, C.S.V.

Background:
Dr. James D. Barry and
Mr. Thomas Adams
(from left to right)

**The 1980
Loyola – Baumgarth Symposium
on Values and Ethics**

Ethics on a
Catholic University
Campus

March 13 and 20, 1980

James D. Barry, editor

*Professor of English
Vice president and assistant
to the president
Loyola University of Chicago*

Loyola University Press
Chicago, 1980

Contents

Preface

The 1980 Loyola-Baumgarth Symposium was made possible by a grant from the John Baumgarth Foundation. This grant will also fund a similar symposium in 1981 as well as various other activities concerned with values and ethics. Those engaged in renewing Loyola's emphasis on values and ethics were heartened when word of this grant from the John Baumgarth Foundation was received. Our thanks to the Baumgarth Foundation.

My effort as editor of the March 13 and 20, 1980, symposium on "Ethics on a Catholic University Campus" has been to preserve the character of the event itself and at the same time to provide the participants with an opportunity to revise their remarks. What you read here is substantially what the original listening audience heard. Yet all presenters, all panelists, and all identifiable questioners have had the opportunity to revise a typescript, and almost everyone took advantage of the opportunity. It was occasionally impossible to identify a questioner; such a person is listed as "Member of the audience." For reasons of space and continuity I have had to omit some parts of the several discussions.

The planning for this symposium was coordinated by Father Joseph Small, S.J. The members of his committee were as follows:

Dr. James Barry
Dr. Gloria Cunningham
Dr. William Donnelly
Dr. Alice Hayes
Father Walter Krolikowski, S.J.
Dr. Julia Lane
Father Thomas McMahon, C.S.V.
Dr. Paul Mundy
Dr. Patricia Werhane

Loyolans are grateful to this committee for mounting such a successful symposium.

Our thanks also to Mr. Robert Rehn, director of media services, and Mr. Gregory Sprague, director of learning centers, for taping the presentations and discussions; to Ms. Arlene Ranalli for transcribing them; and to Ms. Dipti Shah for general assistance. Without the help of these four people I would not have been able to edit this volume properly.

You have here, then, the proceedings of the 1980 Loyola-Baumgarth Symposium on Values and Ethics. The event was warmly greeted by the entire university community, and we are already well along in the planning for the 1981 symposium.

James D. Barry
October 20, 1980
(Anne's twenty-sixth)

Words of Welcome

Father Raymond C. Baumhart, S.J.
President, Loyola University

It is a pleasure to welcome you to the 1980 Loyola-Baumgarth Symposium on the role of ethics at a Catholic university.

Values and ethics have always been of interest to me. My doctoral dissertation was about the attitudes of business people toward values and ethics. I think that this is a most significant symposium, and I'm honored to be able to say a few words of welcome to open it. I believe that this Jesuit and Catholic university should have a continuing concern about values and ethics. I think it has had such a concern, and I am pleased that our interest has been heightened in the past eighteen months. Now let me tell you briefly how we arrived at this point.

At meetings of the University-wide Planning Committee (called UPCOM), we talked about the most significant aspects of the university. There was discussion on the importance of values and ethics to Loyola, a subcommittee worked on the topic, and then UPCOM recommended to the Board of Trustees that special attention be given to values and ethics by the university in the form of a university-wide dialogue. The trustees approved the recommendation enthusiastically. The intention of both UPCOM and the Board was that everyone in the university should get involved, not the academic group alone but staff, administrators, faculty, and students—that all of us should talk about what ethics means in our own divisions. These discussions did take place, and more than a hundred reports were submitted to Dr. James Barry, who has been coordinating this effort. While the discussions were taking place and the reports were being generated, we were able to attract $50,000 from the Baumgarth

Foundation. We are certainly grateful to the officers of the Baumgarth Foundation for enabling us to have not only this symposium but also a similar event next year and other activities concerned with values and ethics.

We are, then, moving ahead with a renewed emphasis on values and ethics. As you listen to the presentations, I ask you to keep certain questions in mind. Are we satisfied with the way we have institutionalized values and ethics at Loyola, and how are we going to institutionalize values and ethics on all levels? I think and I hope that, when we finish this symposium, the spirit will be a little like that at the Transfiguration. If you recall the Gospel, Peter was so excited about the whole thing that he said, "Let's put up three tents here." What are we going to do after these sessions? What kind of tents are we going to put up? What are we going to do by way of permanent committees, ideas for the future, ways of making Loyola better in this very important area?

Finally, I am very grateful to the participants who have prepared this meeting and who will help us to think through some of these very important matters. Again, welcome to the 1980 Loyola-Baumgarth Symposium.

**Ethics on a
Catholic University Campus**

PANEL 1
Dr. Robert J. Pollock, Jr.,
Dr. Francis Fennell,
Dr. William Hunt,
Father Robert F. Harvanek, S.J.,
Dr. Gerald Gutek
(from left to right)

Ethics in Higher Education:
Encountering All Its Aspects
Father Robert F. Harvanek, S.J.

Moderator:
Dr. Gerald Gutek
Panelists:
Dr. Robert J. Pollock, Jr.
Dr. Francis Fennell
Dr. William Hunt

OVERVIEW
Father Thomas F. McMahon, C.S.V.

An overview of a project might be compared to a photograph of scenery. As a photograph provides the material for viewing relationships among sky, trees, water, land, mountains, and roads, an overview attempts to show which topics were selected for the symposium, why they were chosen, and how they relate to one another. An overview of the 1980 Loyola-Baumgarth Symposium should thus photograph the ethical stature of Loyola University as an urban university that is Christian, Catholic, and Jesuit.

This symposium is the final project of the 1979–80 year of ethics established by Father Raymond Baumhart, S.J., President of Loyola University. For the symposium, Dr. James Barry, Associate Vice-President for Academic Programs, called for papers on the theme of ethics at Loyola. Over forty faculty and staff members responded to the call by submitting abstracts that covered a spectrum of ethical issues. Using a blind evaluating technique, a multicollege committee selected papers that appealed to theoretical as well as applied ethical issues. The theoretical topics raised such questions as "What is ethics?" and "How does ethics at a Catholic university differ from ethics at non-Catholic universities?" Abstracts on applied ethics covered such issues as "Should ethics grow as education progresses?" "Can ethical growth be measured on a Catholic campus?" and "How does helping others apply to the community of an urban, Catholic university?"

The topics for this first of two sessions are theoretical. Father Robert Harvanek, S.J., will discuss the basic concepts that underlie ethical theory. Dr. John Rastovac will cover the idea of ethical growth within a Catholic campus community. Selected panelists will react to each of these papers.

The second session (next week) will treat the problems of applied ethics. First, student panelists will present formal papers on such personal topics as honesty and cheating during examinations and helping the less fortunate. Second, administrators and faculty will voice their concern over the practices of professional groups—legal, medical, dental, social, and business. They will also raise issues that go beyond their codes of professional ethics. The material for applied ethics will thus cover two specific aspects: first, ethical issues that the students consider pertinent; second, ethical practices that relate to professional codes of ethical behavior.

The balance of theory and practice for the two sessions should give insight into the ethical values that the Loyola community—administrators, faculty, students, and staff—reflects and postulates. This 1980 Loyola-Baumgarth Symposium should then provide the photographic setting that portrays lights, shadows, and various colors and shading of ethics at an urban, Christian, Catholic, and Jesuit university.

Dr. Gutek: Thank you, Father. It is my pleasure to moderate the first panel on values and ethics and to introduce the panelists. I'm Gerald Gutek, Professor of Foundations of Education and History and Dean of the School of Education. At the far right is Dr. Robert J. Pollock, Jr., Professor of Oral Biology in the Loyola University School of Dentistry. He received his D.D.S. from Northwestern University and his

2

Ph.D. in oral biology from Loyola University. A member of the Chicago and Illinois Dental Societies, the American Dental Association, the International Association for Dental Research, and the American Association for the Advancement of Science, Dr. Pollock has published research studies and articles in journals in his field. When our panelists present their reactions, you'll be hearing from Dr. Pollock.

Seated next to Dr. Pollock is Dr. William Hunt, Emeritus Professor of Psychology at Loyola University. He holds his B.A. degree from Dartmouth and his M.A. and Ph.D. from Harvard. He is currently engaged in a foundation-sponsored study of higher education. He was awarded the Illinois Psychological Association's 1978 award for outstanding contributions to psychology and the American Psychological Association's 1979 award for distinguished contribution to public service. The author of many books and articles in his field, Dr. Hunt was formerly editor of *Psychology in the School.*

To my far left is Dr. Francis Fennell, Associate Professor of English at Loyola University. He received his Ph.D. from Northwestern University. He has written articles on Victorian literature and on the teaching of writing. Dr. Fennell is the author of *Writing Now* and is the editor of the *Rossetti-Leland Letters,* published by Ohio University Press in 1978.

Now it is a great pleasure for me to present our featured speaker, Father Robert F. Harvanek of the Society of Jesus. Father Harvanek received his B.A. and M.A. degrees from Loyola University of Chicago and his Ph.D. in philosophy from Fordham. He has been a teacher at the secondary and higher levels. He taught Latin and Greek at Loyola Academy and was Professor of Philosophy at Loyola's West Baden College. He is currently Chairman and Professor of Philosophy at Loyola University. He is a member of the Jesuit Philosophical Association, the American Philosophical Association, and the Metaphysical Society of America. He is a prolific author who has contributed articles to such journals as *Classical World, Thought,* the *International Philosophical Quarterly, The Review for Religious,* and *The Modern Schoolman.* He has been general editor of the Library of Living Catholic Thought. Father Harvanek is eminently qualified, as you can see from his credentials, to present the first paper in the 1980 Loyola-Baumgarth Symposium on Values and Ethics. He is going to give us a philosophical perspective that will guide us in our exploration of values in higher education. So it is my pleasure to present to you Father Robert Harvanek, who will speak on "Ethics in Higher Education: Encountering All Its Aspects."

Ethics in Higher Education: Encountering All Its Aspects
Father Robert F. Harvanek, S.J.

Fundamental Distinctions in Ethics

Understanding is a matter of distinctions. If an issue is to come clear, it is necessary to sort out, or analyze, the different aspects of the problem, then deal with them in a sequential fashion (order), and finally put them together in a comprehensive response (synthesis). Otherwise discussion or debate is simply a helter-skelter expression of opinions that pass each other without meeting.

This principle is verified, perhaps preeminently, in discussions about ethics and values, and very much so in discussions about ethics and values in higher education.

This paper deals with distinctions—the fundamental distinctions to be made in discussing ethics and values in higher education. It will attempt to lay out five such distinctions that ought to be considered in any discussion of ethics and values in the university.

To distinguish is to define. Both operations depend upon a point of view. My own point of view will undoubtedly become clear as I proceed, but there is no reason to keep it a secret. It is possible, of course, that I misread myself, but insofar as I understand myself, let me say that my point of view is that of a personalist in the classical metaphysical tradition.

Value and Moral Value

The symposium speaks of both ethics and values, as does the university's program in ethics and values. It is possible, of course, that the symposium and the university are using the terms as synonyms. It is possible also, as is sometimes done, to

4

consider ethics as the theory of values and response to values. But there is another important distinction that needs to be made, and that is the distinction between value and moral value.

For not every value is a moral value. There are other values, as, for example, economic values, artistic values, religious values, and the university is dedicated to many of them, especially the intellectual values of inquiry, discovery, knowledge, studiousness, scientific responsibility, intellectual honesty. There is, of course, a moral dimension to these values, but of themselves they are not moral values.

Value is obviously the broader term. There are two traditions in the understanding of value. (In Anglo-American philosophy, this is known as the fact-value or the is-ought distinction.) One tradition places value subjectively within the human evaluator, either socially or individually. A social theory will say that value is the product of an historical social group, which imposes its values on the individual. In this view values are culturally induced. The individualist theory will say that any stirring of interest or desire on the part of the individual creates a value for that individual. From this point of view value is perhaps most broadly defined as "any object of interest" (Ralph Barton Perry).

This definition sounds very much like Aristotle's definition of the good as "that which all desire" (*Nicomachean Ethics*), but there is a difference. For Aristotle there are desires that arise out of the natures of things, in such a way that there is an intrinsic natural relation between the nature and what it desires. The living organism, for instance, desires appropriate nourishment. The empiricist formula makes no such affirmation but simply acknowledges the existence of desires or interests.

The other tradition locates value in the object. In this view the object is good-in-itself. This does not mean that it is cut off from desire or interest, but rather that desire or interest is roused by the good of the object, instead of the desire or interest making the object good. In the Platonic tradition the good-in-itself speaks to me, and it speaks in a commanding way. It lays an obligation on my freedom; it cannot be ignored. Dietrich von Hildebrand identifies it with the important and contrasts it with the indifferent—that which does not speak to me at all, does not command me, is not important.

There is no one way in which the value-object is explained. Platonists, for instance, place it in the realm of the intentional, that is, the realm of the idea. Aristotelians, on the other hand, locate it within the realm of being, or whatever is, and argue that every being, insofar as it is being, is good (has value).

But the question is: Within this category of the important, of value, where are moral values located? What are moral values? This is one of the intriguing questions of contemporary discussion, though it is by no means a new question.

One tradition, largely biblical in origin and theological in development (Ockham), locates moral values within the will of God exclusively. It is God's command that speaks to my freedom and places an obligation on my will. Another tradition (Aristotelian-Thomistic) places moral values within human nature and says that human nature conceived in all its relationships is the norm of morality.

In this Aristotelian tradition the specifically moral rests on the distinction between man as man (*anthropos* = man/woman) and man's functions as mechanic, housekeeper, teacher, etc. There is then an area of value that touches the very essence of the human being; it either affirms that essence or negates it. To the extent that it does either, it is morally good or evil. Supplementary human functions may be ordered to the central human value, or they may add to it, but they are not the heart of the matter. To be a farmer has its value, and it is necessary for human sustenance, but not everyone need be a farmer. Everyone, however, must be just, and courageous, and temperate, and wise. These touch the inner core of the human as human.

A contemporary version of this "human-nature" tradition is expressed in personalist terms: "Moral as the opposite of amoral or nonmoral refers to all judgements of *what befits or does not befit persons as persons*" (Daniel C. Maguire, *The Moral Choice,* p. 71).

This is close to my own formula: *Moral is whatever contributes to the growth of persons as persons in community.* There is a certain redundance to this formula, since in my understanding "person" already includes other persons. It is distinguished from the individual (*indivisum in se et divisum a quolibet alio*; cf. also Descartes and Kierkegaard), an atomic conception, a being that is unrelated, cut off from every other. A person is someone who speaks to another, face to face (*persona/prosopos*), who is in communication with another.

It is communication that defines a person, but not any communication, only that communication that has a free and intellectual component. It is difficult to define these elements, and it is impossible within the limits of this presentation. Let me simply say that free communication is self-initiating communication and that it is not completely determined by other causes. It is, moreover, dependent upon the intellectual power. The intellectual power in its turn is what raises the person above the merely empirical and the particular and into the realm of meaning and free response. The intellectual component opens up the human to a universe other than the universe of sense and matter. It is the personal universe, in which men and women, races and cultures, communicate with one another, with the realm of the angels, and with God.

The formula also conceives the human person as always in development either towards or away from its own idea. Every free action either enhances or diminishes the person as person. This is the sphere of the moral. But it is necessary to remember that the personal includes the community of persons. Thus, that is morally good which contributes to the growth of persons in community; that is morally evil which is destructive of the personal and of the community of persons.

It is perhaps easier to identify the immoral, and perhaps that is why moral imperatives are generally expressed in negative statements: Thou shalt not . . .

This question of the specification of the moral is one of the central issues of current ethical discussion (cf. Kurt Baier, *The Moral Point of View*). I mention only the position that the moral dimension arises only where there is conflict of wills (John Macmurray, *Persons in Relation,* p. 116). My view places morality in the value that posits a norm for free choice.

Knowledge and Virtue

The distinction between knowledge and virtue is probably the best known in the field of education and the one most appealed to even today. It became famous because of Socrates' (Plato's) position that knowledge is virtue and that no one knowingly does evil. This was countered by Aristotle's distinction between intellectual and moral virtue and the associations of moral virtue with the passions of the soul rather than with the mind. Aristotle's analysis, even though he ultimately interrelates both virtue and knowledge, not only allows for the position that high gifts of intellect do not always go together with high virtue, but also explains the phenomenon that virtuous persons may not have the gifts of science and knowledge.

Catholic and Jesuit educational theory has tended to make both—knowledge and virtue—the twin goals of the educational process. However, until recently this theory has been given a developmental perspective, according to which the positions of the two goals shift as the student progresses from early education to higher education. In early education a great deal of attention is paid to education in virtue. But as the child progresses through secondary and collegiate education, the goal of education in virtue recedes, until at the university level almost exclusive attention is given to education in knowledge.

A strong influence on this conception of Catholic education has been John Cardinal Newman's *The Idea of a University,* written with a view to creating a climate for the establishment of a Catholic university in Ireland that would be accepted by the university world. In this situation Newman emphasized that the idea of a university is the pursuit of truth. This has encouraged some proponents of Catholic higher education to maintain that virtue is not the direct concern of the university but of the home and parish, and that the only purpose and goal of the university community is the expansion and communication of knowledge.

In the debate about the cognitive purpose of higher education a distinction is used that is not always made explicit. It is one thing to say that the goal of the university is the expansion or pursuit of knowledge, and another to say that its goal is the pursuit of truth. Though in one sense knowledge and truth are the same thing, in another sense knowledge emphasizes the discovery of new knowledge, is compatible with the empirical and pragmatic mentality, and is not necessarily concerned about the unity and totality of all knowledge. Truth, on the other hand, is concerned about the unity of theory and reality and about the totality of knowledge on all levels. Thus, in a Catholic context the pursuit of truth is frequently understood to include religious and revelational truth and the unity of all knowledge in "the Truth." This, of course, introduces the value dimension into the university.

In the scientific world in our times, the Enlightenment position is that science is value free and should be—natural as well as social and behavioral science. There have been many challenges to that position in recent times from within the sciences themselves. However, the greatest challenge to knowledge as the single goal of the university has been the recent developments in the public domain, starting with the creation of atomic energy and power in the world of physics and going on to the Watergate affair in the profession of law and to the Medicaid scandals and abortion and surgery mills in medicine. A highly trained scientific person without a concomitant development of his/her moral ethical life and judgment is being seen as a monster, of greater danger to the human family than a scientifically ignorant person.

Let me take the eudaimonistic position here, so as not to leave the question of the relation between knowledge and virtue without any response.

In my judgment, the eudaimonistic position is not included in the common division of ethical theories between the teleological and deontological. Though teleological, eudaimonism is neither utilitarian nor simply consequentialist. Again, the difference is that eudaimonism expresses an understanding of human nature/person as ontologically possessing a desire for fulfillment that is ultimately human happiness. Again, the position is Greek. In the judgment of Kierkegaard, all Greek philosophy is ethical. By this he means that the pursuit of philosophy (wisdom) among the Greeks was an expression of the fundamental search for happiness in the human person. This would mean that the profound motivation of all search for knowledge, on all levels and in all areas, is a desire for a higher level of existence than that given to us now. (Consider our contemporary myths of life on other planets, space travel, and other types of communities.) If this is true, and I think it is, then all pursuit of knowledge is situated within the total aspiration of the human person and so is coherent with his or her moral and religious life. In fact, in the neoplatonic view virtue—that is, moral virtue—is a condition for the progress of knowledge to the higher levels of existence.

In the other direction it is frequently argued that knowledge does not produce a virtuous person, and, consequently, that it does not help to study ethics as an academic discipline. This position arises whenever there is a question of requiring the study of ethics, e.g., in a core curriculum. In brief response, it can be conceded that Plato's position that knowledge is virtue is extreme. On the other hand, what Plato did prove, it seems to me, is that there is no virtue without knowledge, and that ethical knowledge contributes both to the clarity of ethical decision and to the motivation that is essential to virtue. That is why the Greco-christian tradition includes prudence as an essential and primary element in moral virtue.

Morality and Religion

Another distinction that needs to be made, especially in a church-related university, is the distinction between morality and religion.

There is, it seems, a popular tendency to identify the two. For many, it seems, to be Christian means to be ethical. This is perhaps the case with Catholicism more than with other institutional religions because the Church claims and exercises authority over both faith and morals. One can get the impression from student responses that Catholicism is a matter simply of moral obligations (keep the Commandments and go to Mass on Sunday, where "going to Mass" is seen as simply another commandment, that is, of the Church), and not an expression of our situation as fallen creatures.

It is true that all the major religions do have a moral code as part of their total religious stance, and perhaps one or other of them (Confucianism) may be primarily ethical systems. Nevertheless, it is possible to distinguish what is specifically religious from the ethical dimension of the human person. This is expressed in Kierkegaard by his analysis of the stages of life's way into the aesthetic, the ethical, and the religious.

However, the distinction is not easily made within the Judaeo-Christian (and Islamic) tradition, since the ethical, from the days of the Pentateuch, is seen as having its origin in the majesty and dominative power of the Creator. The worship of God is obedience to His commandments. Thomas Aquinas, too, places religion and ethics together, for he locates the virtue of religion among the moral virtues, under justice. Religion in this view is a response to the just claims of the Creator upon the creature. "He made us, we belong to Him" (Psalms 100).

The Christian tradition, in particular, is moreover eschatological. That is, it relates everything in human life to the kingdom of heaven, and it relates the present life to the future life. It is true that in recent times Catholic culture has been experiencing an "incarnationalist" phase; that is, it has been emphasizing the entrance of God into our world in Christ and has been arguing that the "kingdom of heaven is among us" and that the kingdom of heaven is a work of history as well as of eschatology. Nevertheless, the Christian spirit tends to lift the eyes of the mind to heaven.

But there are forces at work in our times that distinguish ethics from religion. There is, of course, the effort of the secular humanists of our culture who are reluctant to admit that there can be no ethics without religion. Further, the general religious pluralism of American society influences ethicists to develop their ethical positions independently of religion. In this context even philosophers who are Catholics (e.g., Germaine Grisez, *Beyond the New Morality*) argue their case without appealing to religious data.

How, then, are religion and ethics to be distinguished? Religion is a relation of the human to a world and a reality that transcends the physical-perceptual world we experience. Ethics is our relation to other persons in this world and to ourselves as persons in this world.

A contemporary French writer, Jean-Claude Barreau, distinguishes religion and ethics. He writes: "When I speak of the religious fact, I mean man's/woman's instinct, impulse, and disposition for adoration" (*The Religious Impulse,* p. 16). He goes on to say: "It must be forcefully said, however, that religion is not ethics. . . . For my part, I have never asked any clergyman to make my ethical decisions for me" (p. 45).

That second position may be a little extreme, but it does contain an element of truth. A priest as priest is centrally a leader of prayer and worship (Vatican Council II). It is only by virtue of his role as a guide of souls in the way of the spirit that the ethical dimension enters his perspective. Not every priest is a competent ethicist, and, of course, not every competent ethicist is a priest.

Barreau characterizes ethics as an affair of common sense, situation, and circumstance (p. 45). By this characterization he means to distinguish ethics from the religious impulse to the transcendent. It might be said that, whereas religion expresses a vertical dimension in human existence, ethics expresses a horizontal dimension. Ethics faces out toward the other, towards other human persons. That is why it sometimes seems to be wholly absorbed in the realm of justice. Even when charity is added to justice as the formal element of ethics, the direction is still interpersonal, toward the other. It does not directly relate to higher, eschatological existence. It exists rather in the middle plane, as in Kierkegaard's pattern, between the aesthetic life and the religious life.

Of course, the Catholic religion does consider morals an essential part of its way. It makes another distinction, however, which is worth noting here—the distinction between moral theology, or revelational ethics, and philosophical ethics. It is distinctive of Catholic Christianity that it recognizes the capacity of philosophical reason to work out a human ethics that is valid in its own right and is coordinate with revelational ethics. It used to be the common view that aside from specific religious obligations (the Sacraments) and the laws of the Church, the only difference in principle between philosophical ethics and theological ethics lay in the Christian conception and law of charity. Today, however, many theologians teach that the major religions all have a comparable law of love and that what specifies Christianity is only the motivation and power (grace) provided by Jesus Christ.

This distinction lies behind the Catholic position on such questions as the indissolubility of marriage, birth control, and abortion. These, in the Catholic understanding, as in many other ethical positions, are not simply a matter of Catholic faith, but of human reason. Consequently, they do not represent the imposition of a Catholic ethics upon human society but an argument that these ethical positions are proper to human understanding wherever it is found.

Of course, the question is not simple. What the Catholic stance adds to the philosophical is the dimension of authority (Gerard J. Hughes, S.J., *Authority in Morals*), an authority extrinsic (but cf. Maurice Blondel) to philosophy, an authority that both reinforces certain philosophical positions and selects out those philosophical positions over others that are coordinate with revelation in Christ.

Naturally, a tension develops when actual philosophical reason does not arrive at conclusions that the Church authorities understand to be the correct positions. In this situation philosophy is granted extraordinary power in the sphere of ethics and, at the same time, is put under extraordinary constraint. The situation also raises the question of Christian ethics—whether this is theological ethics or philosophical or both. It also raises the question of the nature of theological ethics vis-à-vis philosophical ethics and of whether theological ethics is necessary for the guidance of Christian conscience. The actual situation is that Catholics generally go to theologians for their ethics, and the irony is that the theologians are generally doing philosophy.

It is important, however, in a Catholic university to ask whether philosophical ethics is enough.

Learning and the Climate of Learning

Earlier we considered the distinction between knowledge and virtue. One position in that context is that knowledge is independent of virtue; it has its own dynamisms and its own norms. This position relates to another that is significant in all education, especially institutional education—the distinction between learning and the climate of learning. Is it proper, if possible, to concentrate the entire learning process on instruction, the classroom and the library, and not be concerned about the context of learning? Or is it necessary to pay attention to the social, psychological, and even religious ambience/environment in which the learning activities take place?

There probably is no disagreement with the view that there can be conditions that inhibit study and learning. Some are frequently mentioned at Loyola: noise in library and dormitory, the pragmatic spirit, academic dishonesty, excessive competition, fear, excessive involvement, lack of role models, unclear signals from the university structures and processes, and others. But there is not the same consensus about the importance of a healthy and happy social atmosphere, a generally ethical attitude of justice and charity, and a religious spirit of prayer and worship, not only for total human development but also for the learning process itself.

This distinction is commonly institutionalized in the two, or three, worlds of the academic faculty, student personnel services, and university ministry. Student personnel services and university ministry see themselves, I believe, as part of the total educational process of the university. But it is not evident that these departments of the university understand themselves as underpinning and supporting the cognitional enterprise of the university.

Behind this situation is an implicit theory of intellect and knowledge and their relation to the other dimensions of the human person. At one end of the spectrum of possible positions, intellect and knowledge (the mind) are conceived as isolated and independent powers and functions that are self-initiating and self-motivating. They can be interfered with by other activities and influences, but their optimum situation is to be allowed to function alone (Enlightenment philosophy?). At the other end is the theory that mind exists only to satisfy human desire and emotions (Hume) or the needs of human action (James, Marx).

Somewhere in the middle is the position that mind arises out of lower stages of human dynamics (physical, vital, sentient, rational, interpersonal) and that mind itself has levels of interest and activity (*ratio inferior, superior*). The highest of these mental activities reaches beyond itself to a higher order of reality (*Deus semper maior. Capax entis, capax Dei*). This is a developmental view of the human person that harmonizes with contemporary psychological theory (Erikson, Kohlberg) as well as with contemporary spiritual theory (J. G. Bennett, *A Spiritual Psychology*).

The last two theories should lead to the practical conclusion that it is most healthy for human knowledge to rise to the context of the total human person in its social, psychological, and religious relationships.

I have left the definition of learning unclarified, whether it means the process of learning or the content of learning. This has perhaps been subconsciously intentional, because I do not know how significant that distinction is. Except in very formal reflection, it may be difficult to separate content and method. I am inclined to agree with Aristotle, who maintained that every content has its appropriate method. I suppose the converse of that may also be true: Every method has its appropriate content.

An instance may illustrate the problem: Consider the interesting question of the causes that brought about or made possible the rise of empirical science in the West—that is, not only why it surfaced in Renaissance Europe, but also why it surfaced only there. According to one theory (Enlightenment), science arose because the search for knowledge broke free of the domination of revelational religion, because the Renaissance reintroduced the pre-Christian humanistic ideal of inquiry. But another theory roots the growth of western science in the Judaeo-Christian theology of an intelligent Creator of a universe distinct in reality from Himself, and of a Creator of the human person as a second creator, an image of Himself. There are other suggestions that the scientific nisus in the West rises out of the medieval spirit of contemplation (Jean Leclercq, O.S.B., *The Love of Learning and the Desire for God*) and that the devotion of early scientists, not to mention later scientists, had a religious dimension. And it is arguable that the dynamism of the Society of Jesus in the areas of science and the arts was and is energized by its commitment to "the greater glory of God."

The University and the City
The distinction between town and gown has been with us ever since the rise of the university in the Middle Ages. (Consider the most recent replay of this classic confrontation in the movie "Breaking Away.") This distinction, however, is not simply a matter of the tension between the local community of permanent inhabitants concerned about home and prosperity and the transient community of scholars with other interests and needs. The distinction masks a deeper difference between the interests of the university and the interests of the local community. The university has traditionally, at least in the United States, seen itself as asocial and apolitical. The city and nation are, of course, both social and political.

Positively, this means that the university sees its sole concern to be the unrestricted desire to know and the desire to communicate what it knows. It sees itself as neither the instrument of social and political forces nor as directly concerned with them. We are again at the value-free position.

There are a number of considerations that tend to modify this simple expression of difference and contrariety between university and community.

First of all, though the interests of students and of parents may be individualist and concerned primarily with the individual prosperity of those who enter the university process as learners, the university itself is established and sustained by social groups because of its value for these groups. This is obviously the case with state-supported universities and church-related universities. I believe it is the case also with the so-called private universities; they, too, are supported and sustained not by the students and parents alone, but by those who wish to foster a different kind of social value than that promoted by the state or the church.

Secondly, not everyone within the university sees the university as unrelated to the social and political structures of society. There are those who consider the functions of the university to include that of being a critic of actual structures and operations of government and of social and economic society. To be apolitical in this point of view means to be free of the actual reigning ideology, not simply to be its slave.

This mentality has been even expressed in recent discussions of Catholic universities vis-à-vis the Catholic Church. In this view, the Catholic university exists not simply to be an expression of the ethos and actual teaching of the hierarchy (*magisterium*) of the Church, but also, as part of its serious responsibility, to be a critic of the Church and its practices and teaching.

Thirdly, critics of the apolitical stance of some university people point out several fallacies in that position. One is that those who claim an apolitical position are blind to an implicit but real ideology that is at work in the academic establishment. Revolutionary interests frequently find the university to be committed to the status quo, to be a communicator of the value system of established society, and to be preparing students for entrance into the Establishment.

The second criticism is that the direction of scientific and intellectual inquiry is frequently governed by extrascientific forces, such as the availability of resources, especially financial resources; the interests of the market place; the particular interests of the practitioners; the spirit of the times; the dynamics of new discoveries; and so on. This suggests that the pure desire to know is an abstraction and never really exists. It is better to be reflectively aware of these influences and to acknowledge them than to deny them naively.

Finally, the developments of academia inevitably and in the long run do have an impact on society. This is most obvious in the realm of science and technology, but it is also true in the realm of the arts and of social studies.

These considerations, it seems to me, lead to the conclusion that the university is indeed a social agent, and that it has a responsibility to society and to history ("The Church Today," #55, *The Documents of Vatican II,* edited by Walter M. Abbott, S.J.). The question is whether the university should explicitly acknowledge this responsibility and direct its research and its teaching to include in a significant way the development of a more human and more just society. For the university does have choices; it is not merely a collection of impulses or unfree dynamics.

It does not follow from this that the university should be directly active in the social and political arena (after the manner of the "students" in Iran). This would conflict with its proper activity, which is the search for knowledge and wisdom and the development of socially responsible persons.

Thus, though the university indeed is distinct from the city, it is distinct not as one of two competing social groups, but as a part of the whole, and a very important, even essential, part. The university is one of the agents for the production of the city of man. If it is a Christian university, then it is also an agent for the development of the city of God.

This last consideration of the relation of the university to the city is peculiarly a Jesuit consideration, for the Society of Jesus today sees all of its endeavors as engaged "in the crucial struggle of our time; the struggle for faith and that struggle for justice which it includes" (The 32nd General Congregation of the Society of Jesus, "Jesuits Today").

This consideration is likewise most proper to Loyola University of Chicago, which identifies itself not simply as a university, but as a Catholic, Jesuit, and urban university.

Dr. Gutek: Thank you very much, Father Harvanek. You raised some fundamental questions and issues for us that will be explored here this afternoon and again next Thursday. Let me refer these distinctions that you raised to our panelists. Each panelist is going to comment briefly on Father Harvanek's paper. We'll begin with Dr. Robert Pollock.

Dr. Pollock: When I received a message from Dr. Barry asking me to participate in this symposium on values and ethics in higher education, I wondered whether my background as a dentist, member of the healing arts, faculty member of the medical center, and basic scientist might so color my thoughts that they would be inappropriate at a symposium for the general university. I wondered if my thoughts on values and ethics might apply, not to higher education in general, but only to higher education for professionals in the healing arts. However, the more I reflected on higher education and the more I reflected on the state of our society, particularly as it relates to the city of Chicago, with which the university is so closely related and identified and upon which we are so dependent, the more I realized that the discussion of values, the discussion of ethics, applies not solely to the healing arts. For all time, values and ethics belong in education, particularly in higher education at all levels and in all areas, because they are apropos of and fundamental to living. Father Harvanek's fine paper on fundamental distinctions in ethics certainly provides us all with a great deal to think about. His philosophical considerations I could not expand upon. I would not be qualified to expand upon them.

I would like to add some thoughts about higher education and how I perceive the relevance of values to it. I think this symposium particularly apropos at this time when we have just concluded a strike by firemen leaving the city unprotected—not just from financial loss, but unprotected in the sense of anguish and physical suffering. A single group has set itself aside from society. We have also recently experienced a strike by teachers who proudly proclaimed themselves as professionals and yet walked out of the schools in spite of court injunctions. When groups act independently and not as a part of society, I think that the discussion of values and ethics in higher education gains new meaning, new appropriateness, new relevance. The world seems to have developed the "me" philosophy. People chase happiness. People chase fulfillment, and the chase seems to be centered on material things, the idea being that, if we gain enough money and enough material goods, we will find happiness. And yet there are continuing symptoms in our society that this does not achieve happiness. We do not achieve fulfillment in this way.

18

Certainly one of the roles of higher education is to prepare us better to meet the demands of society. Many people end up in pursuit of higher education to prepare themselves better for jobs. This is not without virtue. But I believe that we cannot think of higher education solely as a pursuit of more knowledge, either as the increase of knowledge by society or as the acquisition of knowledge by the individual. If this is all there is to higher education, then higher education falls short; it is not fulfilling its true destiny. For higher education must be more than just job training. It must educate people on how to live. Father Harvanek states that ethics is a relation to other persons in this world and to ourselves as persons in this world. Certainly this is true, and our relationship must be one of service, one of giving to others, not simply of receiving. Our fulfillment can come only in serving others, in caring, not in self-service. We will find our rewards in fulfillment. But if this is true, how can it be instilled? How can this be passed on to students? Father Harvanek referred to the argument that knowledge does not produce a virtuous person and consequently that it does not help to study ethics as an academic discipline. Well, as chairman of the Curriculum Committee, I am not sure that I can go totally along with this, particularly in a professional school. But there is at least a thread of truth in it. You cannot instill ethics or values in an individual simply by having him or her learn of their existence. Ethics and values can more truly be taught by the example of service and of compassion and the fulfillment that that service produces. I believe that this is where teachers and educators can pass on values and ethics—by example, by instilling them throughout their teaching and throughout their lives, not simply by expounding on them but by living them. I firmly believe that this must be the destiny of higher education. Higher education must incorporate values and ethics as necessary ingredients, just as vital to it as the expansion of knowledge by society and the acquisition of knowledge by the individual. It is frequently stated today that higher education is in deep trouble, particularly higher education in private institutions. No one who is aware of the climate of society can doubt this. But I think that if higher education at this university encompasses values and ethics, lives them, perpetuates them, passes them on, it can live on. Values must be a vital part in making up the true meaning of higher education at this university.

I hope that what I've said this afternoon is not simply, as Father Harvanek stated in his introduction, a helter-skelter expression of opinions that pass each other without meeting. These are true feelings on my part; I hope they are meaningful to you. Thank you.

Dr. Gutek: Thank you, Dr. Pollock. Now Dr. Frank Fennell will comment.

Dr. Fennell: When Duffy Dougherty was head football coach at Michigan State, he was asked a question that got right to the heart of the matter of values in a university community. "Coach," said a young reporter, "don't you think it would be better if scholarships were based on *need* rather than athletic ability?" "Why, son, they already are based on need," said the coach. "If I don't need a boy, I don't offer him a scholarship!"

Such an exchange gets to the heart of things for two reasons: first, because it raises the important question of *definition* (whose need? whose value?), and second, because it raises the important question of *justice.* Father Harvanek's paper is an excellent beginning to this symposium for many reasons, not the least of which is the way his paper asks us to confront these issues of definition and of justice. In commenting on the paper, I will try to respond to Father Harvanek's remarks on these issues.

Very early in his paper Father Harvanek notes that "to distinguish is to define." In the first section, he distinguishes between values in general and moral values in particular. Of the other values, the ones that are not moral values, Father Harvanek observes that "the university is dedicated to many of them, especially the intellectual values of inquiry, discovery, knowledge, studiousness, scientific responsibility, intellectual honesty." When I hear students and colleagues discuss values as they apply to Loyola University, it is often these other values to which they point; yet the language used for such pointing is often the language appropriate to the *moral* values that Father Harvanek emphasizes.

When I hear students and colleagues talk about values in the university, I find four separate clusters of meaning associated with the term *values.* The first is that *values* means good behavior. Good behavior would include, for example, the avoidance of plagiarism (students) or limiting one's extrauniversity commitments (faculty). This definition has the advantage of reminding us of our obligations. But obligations are of course exactly that: obligations, usually enforced by rules. It is against the rules of this university to plagiarize. It is against the rules of this university for a full-time faculty member to give less than a full-time commitment to his or her job. But I would suggest that following the rules of an institution to which you are contractually bound is not the same as having a commitment to values.

A second meaning assigned to *values* is that successful teaching means encouraging students to address contemporary social questions, questions that always have a moral dimension. This meaning is also important, because it reminds us that knowledge cannot survive in a vacuum. Yet the very words we use to describe this process show our dilemma. Do we not use the word *address* precisely because we have no consensus on solutions? Do we not limit ourselves to adjurations like "Get involved" because we cannot agree on the practical form that involvement should take?

Still another definition of values says that we must be objective when we act as scholars but profess our beliefs when we act as educators. This formulation states two important truths: that scholars can let their prejudices ruin their research, and that professors who do not profess embody an anomaly. But such a view elevates a professional *sine qua non* (objectivity) to the level of a moral absolute. Furthermore, it commits us to schizophrenia in our professional lives. Values become like the old academic robes, something to be donned just for the classroom.

A final cluster of statements says that *values* means an awareness of the moral implications of what we do. This view encourages a heightening of sensitivity and envisions as its goal a person who thinks about the moral consequences of any proposed idea or action. Yet the moment we try to define the moral implications of logarithmic decrements, we see the practical limitations of this approach.

I would contend, however, that the evidence of our commitment to values is independent of what we say in class and independent also of the subject we teach. It is not that some of us *could* inculcate values—it is that we all *do*. To teach is to choose. Like Hamlet, we are all compelled to set our times right, whether we want to or not. In other words, I must beg leave to differ with Father Harvanek's example of the scientist with the undeveloped ethical life, because I believe we all have a fully developed set of values. It is just that some sets of values are terribly, terribly dangerous.

This contention that we all do inculcate values is supported by two kinds of recent research. The first kind is in rhetorical theory. Scholars like Richard Weaver have been establishing the fact that all language is sermonic. Whether we realize it or not, every word we use is value laden. All of us, therefore, are rhetoricians. This is as true of the language of logarithmic decrements as it is of the language of philosophy, theology, or literature. For example, if logarithmic decrements are presented in a tired, dull voice, we convey among other things the message that logarithmic decrements—nay, mathematics itself—is a tired, dull subject. Closer to home, if I teach Tennyson's elegy *In Memoriam* in a manner more befitting the deceased Arthur Hallam than the grief-torn poet himself, I have made a moral statement, whether I realize it or not, and I have betrayed values which I hold dear.

The second kind of research corroborates the first. This research is into the teaching process, into the subtle personal relationships that go on inside and outside the classroom. This research makes it clear that every college teacher willy-nilly acts as a role model for his or her students. It is not that we are what we preach; rather, we preach by what we are—we become existential examples of our own values. Students find in us models for the educated people they are trying to become. When they observe us, the built-in assumption is always "This is what it means to be an educated person." So we must be on our guard lest they find us with the unlit lamp, the ungirt loin. When Father Harvanek talks about the conditions that inhibit or encourage learning, it behooves us to remember that *we* are the conditions.

So we have no choice about transmitting values. That brings us to the second issue: What shall those values be? In a pluralistic world and a pluralistic university, is a consensus on values possible? Here again, with his emphasis on justice—i.e., on "the development of a more human and a more just society"—Father Harvanek has offered some fruitful ideas on the direction in which we can move.

For the sake of discussion, let me offer three propositions that might serve as the basis for a consensus on the nature of our moral commitment. Would it be possible for all of us, no matter what our scholarly discipline or personal creed, to accept these propositions?

First, our goal is to help create men and women whose values are characterized by maturity. Mature values are symbolic values, in order words, values that transcend one's time, place, and social group.

Second, our goal is to help create men and women whose values are rooted in action. In other words, a person must be willing to engage in the painful but rewarding process of finding meaning by choosing, consciously and freely, among alternatives. Then he or she must be willing to express those values publicly and to base his or her actions on them.

Yet we cannot be indifferent to the nature of the values which impel that action. So our third goal is to help create men and women whose values, whatever form they take, are anchored firmly in a devotion to humanity. In Father Harvanek's formulation, that means "whatever contributes to the growth of persons as persons in community." Every important tradition speaks of this imperative. Jesus offers the radical command to love our neighbors as ourselves. The Hasidic master Baal Shem-Tob reminds us that we must see in each person a revelation of God. The Buddhist Khempo of Nyalgal affirms that the only person who is ready for enlightenment is the person who sees the need for the deliverance of all human beings. In short, we must all be what Father Harvanek calls social agents; the task for each of us, then, is to define the practical implications of the role we have already chosen.

A cynic once remarked that values are discussed only when they become moot and questionable. For academic communities, the communities in which we have chosen to spend part or all of our adult lives, that cannot be true. Academic communities have always been bound by the injunction of the ancient Chinese philosopher Hsun Tsu: "He who does not make himself one with righteousness and benevolence cannot be called a good scholar."

Dr. Gutek: Thank you, Dr. Fennell. Now Dr. Hunt.

Dr. Hunt: It seems fitting to me that, as a social scientist, I devote my remarks to one problem that arises throughout Father Harvanek's paper—the popular tendency to separate scientific inquiry from the world of moral values, a separation that I find inappropriate for any institution of higher education.

The difficulty lies in the tendency, as Father Harvanek points out in an earlier working outline of his paper, for the public not only to distinguish between the two fields but also to separate them. Being no philosopher, I turn to the dictionary for help in making the distinction and point out that *to distinguish* means to mark off as different, to recognize the individual features of, whereas *to separate* means to keep apart, to dissociate, to disconnect.

True, scientific inquiry and moral values are distinct and different areas, but they should not be separated, dissociated, and disconnected, as they often tend to be. Rather, they should exist in a functional relationship, complementary to each other, with scientific inquiry furnishing an information base for rational judgment in the area of ethics and morals as well as in the day-to-day, practical affairs of man. I am not saying that the information furnished by scientific inquiry is the only basis for moral judgment, nor in saying that it offers a rational basis am I implying that all other bases are irrational. I am merely stating my belief that the knowledge provided by scientific inquiry can be used in facilitating ethical and moral judgment and can reinforce the moral process rather than disrupt it.

I should like to carry this distinction between distinguishing and separating a bit further. Over the past fifty years, a great deal of my time has been occupied in the investigation of human judgment in all its forms. My studies have ranged from the somewhat arcane specialty of psychophysics, in which experimental psychology got its start, through the practical problems of clinical judgment, including the diagnostic process, to the less objective areas of aesthetics and ethics. These last two I would class as "value" areas, as opposed to the first two, which are more concerned with matters of information-based decision making. My observations have been both experimental and rational.

My experience has led me to three conclusions, the first two of which bear upon the qualitative characteristics of value judgments that distinguish them from the ordinary garden variety of cognitive decisions, while the third bears upon the question of separating the field of values from the realm of ordinary intellectual inquiry, which includes the specialized methodologies of science. I feel that:

1. Value judgments are distinguished by a relative lack of any extensive information base. They seem to be more immediate, more automatic, less cognitive, and justified more by authority than by reasoned consideration. In part I would attribute this to the fact that the child assimilates his values automatically and unconsciously from his family relationships, his peer-group practices, and the cultural environment to which he is subjected. Too often his morals are taught him as authoritative givens, completely outside of any intellectual context.

2. Value judgments are laden with emotion. Much of the conflict between ethics and scientific inquiry is attributable to this. As Father Harvanek states, this is in large part attributable to the fact that values touch very intimate and personal areas of the individual. But there are other causes as well. The individual who has unconsciously and unthinkingly adopted his values on the authority of family or peer group often is hard put to it to justify them in intellectual discussion. This is particularly frustrating when the atmosphere is one of argument.

Moreover, the intimate nature of one's values often touches unresolved personal conflicts and therefore is threatening to one's personal organization and integrity. This is the source of psychology's infamous list of defense mechanisms, and the resolution of such conflicts is the mainstay of psychotherapy. It seems obvious to me that the marriage of emotion and intellect into a harmoniously functioning team is indicated. This leads to my third conclusion.

3. Both the value judgments of aesthetics and ethics and those more pragmatic ones of mathematics, philosophy, and science are mediated by the same mechanisms and reveal common processes of judgment. One finds the same principles at work in every area of decision making, from the quantitative, psychophysiological abstraction of psychophysics to the subjective realities of aesthetic and ethical values. They are both influenced by the range of stimuli or experiences presented to the individual, the context in which these experiences occur, and the availability of reference points (anchoring points). This is as true of a judgment of moral values as it is of the quantitative evaluation of lifted weights in psychophysical measurement.

What has this to do with higher education? The bringing together of the world of scientific inquiry and the world of moral values into a related unity of knowledge has always seemed to me to be the basic purpose of a *uni*-versity. In our haste to satisfy the diverse pragmatic needs of a complex society, we have been unduly distracted by the concept of the *multi*-versity. In the course of distinguishing the many and diverse fields of scholarly endeavor, we have been led by practical concerns into separating them. This is why I object to the description of our educative task as postsecondary education. To me this term conceals or at least overlooks the major goal of higher education: to bring together both the heart and the mind of man in a functioning unity. This is the meaning of *higher* education.

Dr. Gutek: I'd like to raise three issues. It seems to me that what emerges as a broad issue in the paper and in the responses is the theme of persons in community, that is, faculty and students in a university community. If we probe the question of community in the United States and the university as we enter the '80s, I think it is difficult to find the community. Although it appears to exist on the surface, one finds special-interest groups existing below the surface. This is very clear in what Dr. Pollock was alluding to—the recent teachers' strike and firemen's strike. And I think, once we go beneath the surface of university community, we in reality find the multi-versity lurking.

The second issue I'd like to raise is related to the theme of value-free science and ethical scientists. I also see many people here that I would call the managers of the university. It seems that many of the ethical issues in the United States, and perhaps in the universities in the late '60s and early '70s, were ethical decisions on the part of managers, who were neither scientists, teachers, nor students but who managed the institution.

The last question I pose is that of individualism. How can we integrate the historic American sense of individualism and the sense of personalist community that you raised for us, Father? We will now give you a chance to respond, if you'd like, to the panelists or to any of the questions raised.

Father Harvanek: I don't believe there is any need to respond to the comments of the panelists, since I do not see them as challenging my remarks. Rather, they used my paper as an opportunity to contribute additional developments and perspectives. This perhaps confirms the insight of the program committee. The original title of my paper was somewhat modest but dull: "Fundamental Distinctions in Ethics." As it was, I opened up five distinctions, not to mention several subdistinctions, and I was aware that I was really laying the groundwork for several papers. The editor picked this up in retitling the paper: "Ethics in Higher Education: Encountering All Its Aspects."

I certainly concur with the ideas that intellectual knowledge and instruction by themselves are not enough, and that we cannot escape communicating our values. I suppose there can be a question about whether we communicate "good" values as well as "bad" values. This depends of course on whether we limit the use of the word *value* only to "good" values, or whether it is used to cover whatever it might be that governs our choices.

With reference to the question about whether Loyola University is a community, perhaps the sociologists might be able to contribute something towards an answer. A university is certainly a complex community. It is not simply a collection of people in disunity. Nor is the ideal a simple collection of people in unity. It needs perhaps to be conceived as a collection of communities, and of communities on different levels. In an interdisciplinary faculty seminar in which I participated, it was pointed out that a city is just that sort of a collection of interrelated communities on different levels, and I suppose the same model can apply to a university. Perhaps, too, as in a city, so in a university there is a scale of models that stretches between radical democracy and absolute totalitarianism. The ideal republic, I presume, is somewhere in between.

I would like to make a distinction between interpersonal relationships and structures in a society. Interpersonal relationships are not necessarily structured, or they can be minimally structured. But as a community becomes more complex, it becomes more organized and more structured, and there is a danger that the structures will take over and the interpersonal will get lost. That should not be allowed to happen in a university, especially a Jesuit university. One of the dominant themes of Jesuit education from the beginning has been concern for the individual (*cura personalis*). This is directed primarily towards the students, but it relates to everyone within the university community.

The question was asked whether managers in a university, no less than the teachers, have a role to play in the development of ethics and values. There can be no doubt that they do, and an important role, and in many ways. In their own functions they have decisions to make and execute that have ethical dimensions. They play a large part in the appointment of the personnel in the university, including the faculty, and in the last analysis the spirit of a university depends upon its personnel. Moreover, an educational institution teaches by its processes and structures, and management has a great deal to do with these.

Dr. Gutek: Thank you. (*To the audience*) You've been sitting very patiently. I wonder if any of you have any questions that you'd like to direct to Father Harvanek or to the panelists.

Father Donald Hayes, S.J.: I would like to stress the importance of a complementary need. We have spoken much about the teacher as a role model, the value of teaching ethics by example, and I thoroughly subscribe to this. What I think is also essential in an academic institution, however, is that there be a real intellectual understanding of ethics. Dr. Hunt mentioned some of the reasons why we may hold one position rather than another. If we as faculty and staff do not challenge students to an understanding of why they hold a position, why they have this or that ethical stance, and ask them if their position is based on a real conviction and has an intellectual basis, then I think we are failing in our role as educators and as an educational institution. So while I would subscribe heartily to the role-model position, I think that we must also have an intellectual approach to ethics in the classroom.

Dr. Hunt: You would agree with me, I guess, if you don't mind my specialized term, *information base.*

Father Hayes: I am a little concerned that we not simply hold positions but really defend them rationally. For example, in the matter of "conscience," I hope we do not hold a position "because I feel that way" or "society kind of moves me this way." You might take, for example, the tragic case that is in our newspapers—the Gacy case. Why is it we are appalled, why is it that we are morally indignant about this type of behavior? What is our intellectual reasoning? Is it simply because this is contrary to what we usually do, or are there some deeper reasons that are intellectually able to be defended?

Dr. Hunt: I would see both in the Gacy case. It certainly touches all sorts of conflicts in an individual, and it also raises some intellectual questions concerning the practice of murder. If people want to live, it is best they not be murdered. I'm putting that very simply, but I think we're in agreement.

Father Hayes: My only point is that I think in an academic institution, in a university, if there is not an intellectual and an academic approach to the science of ethics as ethics, then I do not know where ethics is going to be considered professionally. It is not going to be done in the marketplace. It is not going to be done by society in general. I think it is one of the predominant roles of a university to debate, challenge, and hold ethical positions that have both an intellectual content and foundation.

Dr. Hunt: I think Dr. Pollock would also say that one of the interesting things you can do is to teach your students the development of ethical roles in your professions—and there you've got a role model in a somewhat different sense than the one we were using earlier.

Dr. Pollock: Maybe I started this when I quoted Father Harvanek's position (not his position, but what he had quoted) and said that there is a thread of truth in it. There is a thread of truth in the statement that you can't teach ethics solely as an academic phenomenon. Again, as I pointed out, I am also on the Curriculum Committee, and I certainly wouldn't want to have a curriculum in a professional school without a course in ethics, because there are certainly many things that can be brought out in a course in ethics and many aspects of things that can't be gotten at simply by trying to institute ethics in a broad base. But I think that you have not only to teach it but to emulate it and bring it out in other contexts besides specific academic courses.

Father Harvanek: With reference to the question as to whether the "Catholic" character of Loyola University does not add some unique or specific quality to the issue of ethics and values in the university, I did have something to say about that in my paper. There is a growing tendency on the part of Catholic moralists and theologians to say that Catholicism does not add anything specific to the content of ethics. That is, all the principles, attitudes, and positions that are found in the Hebrew-Christian revelation can be found in principle and sometimes actually in other religious traditions. And the Catholic tradition itself has for centuries maintained that most of its specifically ethical positions can be arrived at by strictly philosophical reasoning and are not a matter simply of revelation or religious teaching. This applies to the most controversial items of present-day debate, such as abortion, birth control, and euthanasia.

There is another dimension, however, in which the Catholic element would have an important role to play, and that comes under the heading of the "context of learning." This would involve the sacramental life within the university and the life of worship, the devotion to Christ, and concern for spiritual and religious growth. This does sustain and encourage the ethical spirit and a life of high moral values. Worship was at one time much more a part of the university than it is now. Holy days of obligation were actually holidays. Certainly the public climate has changed, and Loyola and its management has been outstanding in building up a strong and active department of religious ministry, but in some areas we don't do as much as other, non-Catholic institutions do, and we are more shy about expressing our religious ethos than our coreligionists, even those here at Loyola, are.

Dr. Gutek: It's time for us to bring our part of the program to a conclusion. I want to thank you again, Father Harvanek, Dr. Pollock, Dr. Fennell, and Dr. Hunt, for participating.

PANEL 2
Father Bert Akers, S.J.,
Dr. Thomas Wren,
Dr. Patricia Werhane,
Dr. John Rastovac,
Ms. Maureen Fuechtmann
(from left to right)

Cognitive and Moral Development: Living Through the Developmental Stages

Dr. John Rastovac

Moderator:
Dr. Patricia Werhane
Panelists:
Ms. Maureen Fuechtmann
Dr. Thomas Wren
Father Bert Akers, S.J.

Father McMahon: This second session will focus on cognitive and moral development. It will be moderated by Dr. Patricia Werhane, Assistant Professor of Philosophy. Dr. Werhane did her undergraduate work at Wellesley College and holds an M.A. and a Ph.D. in philosophy from Northwestern University. She writes in the fields of ethics and the philosophy of art; she is the co-author of *Ethical Issues in Business*; and she is the author of *Art and Nonart*.

Dr. Patricia Werhane: Thank you, Father McMahon. I am very pleased today to introduce Professor John Rastovac, Assistant Professor in the Department of Natural Sciences. Dr. Rastovac is a graduate of St. Vincent's College. He received his Ph.D. from Purdue University in science education and biology. He previously taught at California State and at Purdue. He has published a number of articles in cognitive development, and he is currently working on a book on this subject. He has been at Loyola since 1977. The title of his speech is "Cognitive and Moral Development: Living Through the Developmental Stages." Dr. John Rastovac.

Cognitive and Moral Development: Living Through the Developmental Stages
Dr. John Rastovac

T **The Nature of the Problem**
he idea that cognition and morality undergo stages of development is very reasonable. Observation of other individuals and self-evaluation clearly indicate that a child, an adolescent, and an adult do not think alike, nor do they base their moral behavior on the same ethical principles. In fact, infants and preschoolers seem to lack any semblance of logical thinking and normally are not thought to understand the conventional ideas of right and wrong.

Stages of development in both the cognitive and the moral areas are commonly viewed as in chronological sequence. It also can be asserted that most people, from a general understanding of epistemology, consider the adult pattern of thinking and morality to be the most advanced and preferred stage of development. In such a maturational context, various institutions, such as the family, the church, and the school, are seen as being facilitators of this natural progression. While a nurturing role is logical for these institutions, it is not clear what methods are to be employed. Variance in methodology can lead to variance in end results. Therefore, the selection of a particular methodology involves either an explicit or an implicit value decision.

In the educational setting, therefore, it is necessary to examine the relationship between the conscious activities of the student-teacher interaction and the cognitive and moral development of the student. Central to this analysis are assumptions (possible misconceptions) concerning cognitive and moral education:

1. that morality can be didactically taught as a separate subject and therefore involves a limited number of educators who are concerned with the transmission of socially accepted standards of moral behavior; and

2. that for other educators the involvement is through "the hidden curriculum"; that is, moral instruction will naturally occur as the instructor establishes a norm of acceptable classroom activity (Forisha and Forisha, 1976); or

3. that cognitive development is the maturation of inborn patterns of thought; or

4. that cognitive development is the result of discrete learning experiences; or

5. that cognitive development is a dialectic interaction of organism and environment leading to changes in mental structure.

Clarification of these assumptions can be achieved by examining them in relation to two problems of value theory. The first problem, that of value relativity, simply stated is: Can educational goals, cognitive or moral, be defined whose validity is not based on the needs of a particular individual or culture? The second problem, referred to as "the psychologist's fallacy" (Kohlberg and Mayer, 1972), is concerned with the relation of psychological assumptions about the developmental characteristics of the individual's cognitive and moral structures and the formulation of desirable educational outcomes—"the problem of relating the natural is to the ethical ought" (Kohlberg and Mayer, 1972).

To help resolve these two issues of value theory, three schools of psychological thought and their input into educational ideologies relating to cognitive and moral development will be considered. They are the psychoanalytic, the behaviorist, and the cognitive-developmental. It is the last of these three schools, cognitive-developmental, that will be the major focus for this paper, but first we will briefly examine the other two.

Psychological Schools
The psychoanalytic school, founded on the work of Sigmund Freud, basically holds that man is by instinct driven to seek

pleasure and avoid pain. These instinctive drives reside in the unconscious id. In a communal or societal setting this basic nature of man would lead to conflicts among the members; therefore, a mechanism of restraints is necessary. The restraints are provided by the internally developed and conscious ego and the partially conscious and partially unconscious internalization of cultural norms, the superego. The ego is man's rational power to sort out the pros and cons of a situation in deciding which impulse of the id is to be fulfilled. The fact that the ego is not strong enough at all times to constrain the id explains the need for and existence of the culturally derived superego.

Therefore, according to the psychoanalytic school of thought, moral development occurs through a process of modeling—the superego becomes an internalized model of cultural norms that approves good behavior and causes guilt for bad behavior. Moral education based on this mode of thinking leads to the acceptance of the second assumption (misconception) of the "hidden curriculum" and leaves little room for "formal" classroom moral education (Forisha and Forisha, 1976). Further, by accepting the cultural given as the norm for superego development, we are led into a position of value relativity, and we completely sidestep the question of the relationship between the natural is and the ethical ought, unless we equate the ethical ought with the cultural given.

If the psychoanalytic approach seems doomed to failure in providing a viable basis for an ideology of moral education, why discuss it at all? The foremost reason is that it is implicitly operative in our schooling process. Modeling does occur, whether it be consistent or inconsistent; grades do reflect to a certain extent a system of rewards and punishments; more students are expelled for antisocial behavior than for academic retardation. The viability of the psychoanalytic approach is a separate issue from its influence. It cannot be a viable approach, for it does not address the development of postconventional morality, that is, the development of autonomous moral principles (Kohlberg, 1971).

The Behaviorist School

The classical expression of the behaviorist school of thought that can be gleaned from the writings of Thorndike and Skinner varies in a small degree from the psychoanalytic. While it postulates a neutral versus a slightly negative viewpoint concerning the basic nature of man and the importance of the environment versus internal factors as the determining forces of moral development, it shares with the psychoanalytic approach the acceptance of cultural norms as the basis to guide cognitive and moral development (Forisha and Forisha, 1976).

Kohlberg indicates that behaviorism is the educational psychology associated with the cultural-transmission ideology that is basic to the academic traditions of Western education (Kohlberg and Mayer, 1972):

> Traditional educators believe that their primary task is the transmission to the present generation of bodies of information and rules or values collected in the past; they believe that the educator's job is the direct instruction of such information and rules. The important emphasis, however, is not on the sanctity of the past, but on the view that educating consists of transmitting knowledge, skills and social and moral rules of the culture. Knowledge and rules of the culture may be rapidly changing or they may be static. In either case, however, it is assumed that education is the transmission of the culturally given. (p. 450)

If this is an accurate description of present-day educational practices, then once again we encounter the problem of value relativity. Additionally, this problem becomes enmeshed with the problem of relating "the natural is to the ethical ought," due to the behaviorist viewpoint on the genesis of the cognitively and morally mature individual.

Traditional behaviorists or those who subscribe to newer versions of the cultural-transmission ideology (e.g., Ausubel, 1963; Gagne, 1970) contend that specific concepts and general cognitive structures are reflections of structures to be found in the external environment. Therefore, cognitive development is viewed as a behavioral change induced by instruction, or, simply stated, development from this atomist point of view is the additive result of what is learned. Accordingly, developmental change is reflected in the success rate on content-related exams developed by the instructor. When individual differences in achievement are found to exist, they are thought to result from inborn differences in aptitude for particular types of learning measured by standardized tests, such as mathematics aptitude or SAT (Bloom, 1968). Whether we take an elitist point of view or acquiesce in our decision on what ought to be the developmental goal of education, I believe Bloom aptly describes the result:

> Each teacher begins a new term (or course) with the expectation that about a third of the students will adequately learn what he has to teach. He expects about a third of his students to fail or to just "get by." Finally, he expects another third to learn a good deal of what he has to teach, but not enough to be regarded as "good students." This set of expectations, supported by school policies and practices in grading, becomes transmitted to the students through the grading procedures and through the methods and materials of instruction. The system creates a self-fulfilling prophecy such that the final sorting out of students through the grading process becomes approximately equivalent to the original expectations. (p. 1)

Whether one is an elitist or a conformer to the status quo, the problem of the "psychologist's fallacy" still remains, because we may ask, "Why is it good or desirable to characterize students in this manner? By what standard is that good?" Even if "acceptable" answers to these questions can be formulated and defended, one theoretical question remains: Have we correctly defined cognitive structure and cognitive development? To make a decision on this question, it will be necessary to examine the cognitive-developmental psychology and the empirical evidence presently available pertinent to the question, "What is the relationship between learning and development?"

The Cognitive-Developmental School
Cognitive-developmental psychology is associated with the "progressive" ideology that "developed as part of the pragmatic functional-genetic philosophies of the late nineteenth and early twentieth centuries" (Kohlberg and Mayer, 1972). As with the cultural-transmission ideology, there is an emphasis on knowledge. However, knowledge is not viewed by the progressive ideology as the immediate and recognizable change in behavior evoked by a particular learning experience, but rather as a

change in mental structure brought about by a system transformation through which both the object of knowledge and the individual are modified. Therefore, knowledge is not simply a maturational process wherein innate patterns emerge as a result of growth, nor is it simply the additive effect of discrete learning experiences. It is the dialectical result of an active mind redefining a core of mental structures to achieve a better fit between existing structures and the external environment. This reorganization of cognitive structure proceeds through a sequence of stages that define increased levels of epistemic adequacy. Therefore, this progression is a valid educational goal. According to Kohlberg and Mayer (1972):

> Intellectual education in the progressive view is not merely a transmission of information and intellectual skills, it is the communication of patterns and methods of "scientific" reflection and inquiry. These patterns correspond to higher stages of logical reasoning, Piaget's formal operations. According to the progressive, there is an important analogy between scientific and ethical patterns of judgment or problem-solving, and there are overlapping rationales for intellectual and ethical education. In exposing the child to opportunities for reflective inquiry, the teacher is guided by principles of scientific method which the teacher accepts as the basis of rational reflection. Reference to such principles is nonindoctrinative if these principles are not presented as formulas to be learned ready-made or as rote patterns grounded in authority . . . these principles represent developmentally advanced or mature stages of reasoning, judgment, and action. Because they are culturally universal stages or sequences, stimulation to the next step in a natural direction is equivalent to a long range goal of teaching ethical (and intellectual) principles. (p. 475)

If the claim for a universal, invariant sequence of cognitive stages of development can be supported empirically, then the progressive ideology can define educational goals that are not value relative. Further, the appeal to universal ethical principles as principles and not statements of psychological fact that are used to define both educational goals and methodologies frees the progressive ideology from the "psychologist's fallacy." To examine these claims demands a further examination of structuralism and Piaget's theory of cognitive development.

Piaget's Structuralist Theory of Cognitive Development

Basic to Piaget's theory is the idea of structure. A structure can be viewed as a system of transformations characterized by wholeness, not as a simple aggregate, because the elements of the whole are subordinate to the rules governing the transformations. They are further characterized by self-regulation (Piaget, 1970). Self-regulation implies, in the cybernetic sense, "perfect" regulation, since errors are excluded before they can occur. Piaget (1970) provides the following example to help clarify these ideas:

> A mathematical group is a system consisting of a set of elements (e.g., the integers, positive and negative) together with an operation or rule of combination (e.g., addition) and having the following properties:
> 1. performed upon the elements of the set, the combinatory operation yields only elements of the set;
> 2. the set contains a neuter or identity element (in the given case, 0) such that, when it is combined with any other element of the set, the latter is unaffected by the combinatorial operation (in the given case, $n + 0 = n$ and, since addition is commutative, $n + 0 = 0 + n = n$);
> 3. the combinatory operation has an inverse in the system (here subtraction) such that, in combination with the former, the latter yields the neuter or identity element $(+ n - n = 0)$;
> 4. the combinatory operation (and its inverse) is associative $([n + m] + 1 = n + [m + 1])$. (p. 18)

From this description it is evident that a real difference exists between behaviorists and cognitive-developmentalists when discussing "cognitive structure." While the former mainly equate stages of development with the understanding of arbitrarily selected content, the latter focus on how an individual thinks about and comes to know the environment in which he/she lives. Therefore thought processes not only develop in relationship to specific content but also become generalizable patterns of thought applicable to new content areas.

In accounting for the genesis of structure, Piaget prefers the construction metaphor. Basic to his idea is the concept that two invariant functions, assimilation and accommodation (the primary rules of transformation), work toward a point of equilibrium (self-regulation) or structure. This rudimentary structure now may incorporate new elements by a process of assimilation, which simply means that new external objects can be perceived under the existing mental structure. However, certain external objects or events do not conform to the system of transformations (the existing mental structure), and accommodation is reached by the construction of a new system of transformation, a new state of equilibrium or self-regulation. However, until accommodation to the next structure occurs, the character of an individual's capability is limited by the existing structures.

Piaget also enumerates four factors that influence the construction of cognitive structures: maturation of the nervous system, experience with the physical environment, social interaction, and equilibration. While each of these is a contributing factor, none is sufficient by itself to explain development. For Piaget, however, the process of equilibration is the fundamental factor and can be viewed as the process by which the first three are kept in balance. As mentioned before, equilibration is an active process by which the structures at any stage are brought into balance. While this self-regulating mechanism clarifies existing structures, it may also expose inconsistencies in the structure, causing the active movement toward a stage of increased epistemic adequacy (Phillips, 1969).

Piaget identifies four stages of cognitive development. (It should be noted at this time that the specification of stage durations or time of expected appearance of the next stage is highly variable. What is not variable—this being the more important point—is the *sequence* of stage appearance. Nor is it possible to skip a stage.) The first stage, the sensory-motor, lasts for approximately the first 24 months. During this period the child constructs the structures of object permanence, sensory-motor space, temporal succession, and sensory-motor causality that are necessary for the development of conceptual reversibility and conservatory operations (Piaget, 1964). A primitive motor construct similar to conceptual reversibility can be seen as a child develops the motor "understanding" and causality associated with the on-off movements of a light switch.

The second stage, the preoperational, is associated with the development of language and representational thought. Although capable of representational thought, the child is still perception-bound and incapable of generalizing from particular situations. No true operations (rules of self-regulation) exist. However, a reconstruction of the sensory-motor structures takes place, and as the process of physical and social decentering reaches completion, the first cognitive operations begin to develop (Piaget and Inhelder, 1969).

The concept of operation as a self-regulating cognitive mechanism is central to Piaget's theory, and he defines it in the following manner (Piaget, 1964):

> To know an object, to know an event, is not simply to look at it and make a mental copy or image of it. To know is to modify, to transform the object, and to understand the way the object is constructed. An operation is then the essence of knowledge; it is an interiorized action which modifies the object of knowledge. . . . But in addition, it is a reversible action; that is, it can take place in both directions, for instance adding or subtracting, joining or separating. . . . Above all, an operation is never isolated. It is always linked to other operations, and as a result is always a part of the total structure. (pp. 176–177)

Two types of operations exist, the concrete and formal; therefore the third stage, the operational stage, is accordingly dichotomized into the concrete-operational and formal-operational periods.

According to the theory, concrete operations develop when the child is between the ages of seven and eleven. These operations are termed concrete because they operate on objects and not on verbally expressed hypotheses (Piaget, 1964). Concrete mental structures are self-regulated by class-inclusion operations and serial-ordering operations and thus represent a means for structuring immediately present reality (Inhelder and Piaget,

1958). The concept of reversibility is a landmark characteristic of this period. It leads to the mental operation of conserving physical quantities such as length, weight, and volume, which are the bases for diagnostic assessment.

During the formal-operational stage, the adolescent begins to develop the adult pattern of thinking. Reversibility now includes the reversal of reality and the possible. The most important feature of formal operations is the development of the ability to use hypothetical reasoning based on the logic of all possible combinations and to perform controlled experimentation (Inhelder and Piaget, 1958). In addition, other self-regulating operations are combined into the structured whole, namely, proportional, correlational, combinatorial, and probabilistic reasoning.

To date, there are a number of replication studies confirming the universal, invariant sequence of cognitive stage development proposed by Piaget. Studies by Brainerd (1971), Elkind (1961), and Goldschmid (1967) all confirm Piaget's earlier findings (Piaget and Inhelder, 1940) that conservatory operations show a linear progression in terms of difficulty. Specifically, conservation of number and of liquid and solid amount appear first and indicate early concrete-operational thought, while conservation of length, area, and weight are indicative of late concrete-operational thought. With the appearance of conservation of volume, the transition to formal operations begins; however, there are no clear-cut linear relationships between the formal tasks, since at this level we are dealing with the structural whole, and interrelationships of a "net type" predominate.

To help resolve the question, "Can learning promote development of formal operations?" we can consider the following statement in relation to structural difference between the concrete- and formal-operation stage:

For man, 50 percent of the total body weight is water, while 60 percent of the lean body weight is water.

Question 1. What conclusion can be derived from this statement?

Question 2. What additional information do you need?

Question 3. What percent of the adipose tissue is water?

Both the concrete- and formal-operational student can come to the same conclusion for question 1 by using the classificatory schemata, that is, total body weight = lean body weight + adipose body weight; therefore, total body water = lean body water + adipose body water. For the concrete-operational student, no additional information is required; the answer to question 3 is 40 percent by use of the compensatory schemata, that is, an increase of 10 percent must be accompanied by a decrease of 10 percent to balance the situation. The formal-operational student, however, realizes that this is only true for the case where the total body weight is equally divided between lean body weight and adipose body weight, the "all-other-things-being-equal" schemata. Any deviation requires the use of proportional reasoning. For example, if total body weight = 100 kg, lean body weight = 80 kg, and adipose body weight = 20 kg, then the answer to question 3 is 10 percent. Can such elaborate thought processes result from ordinary class instruction on material that requires these structures? Or does learning depend on the prior presence of these structures?

These questions were examined by Lawson (1973), who studied the understanding of concrete- and formal-operational concepts by concrete- and formal-operational students in high school biology, chemistry, and physics classes. The results of the study indicate that only those students who were classified as formal-operational scored above the chance level for questions requiring formal-operational thought. The general conclusion is that ordinary instruction does not lead to concept development in those areas requiring formal thought unless the student is functioning at this level during the course of instruction. Consequently, an atomist interpretation of structure genesis seems inappropriate.

Kohlberg's Cognitive-Developmental Approach to Morality

According to Kohlberg, a person's ability to make moral judgments is limited by the individual's ability to think rationally. This is based on the assumption that the mechanism for rational morality is the same as for rational thought. Therefore, cognitive development is a necessary, but not sufficient, condition for moral reasoning.

It is not a sufficient condition because moral-judgment stages are not purely cognitive, i.e., permitting the application of logic to moral questions. Kohlberg expresses the relationship between cognitive and moral development in the following manner (Kohlberg and Gilligan, 1972):

> In Piaget's and our view, both types of thought and types of valuing (or of feeling) are schemata which develop a set of general structural characteristics representing successive forms of psychological equilibrium. The equilibrium of affective and interpersonal schemata, justice or fairness, involves many of the same basic structural features as the equilibrium of cognitive schemata logicality. Justice (portrayed as balancing the scales) is a form of equilibrium between conflicting interpersonal claims, so that in contrast to a given rule imposed upon the child from outside, the rule of justice is an imminent condition of social relationships, or a law governing their equilibrium. (pp. 163–164)

Therefore, the formation of mental structures about moral problems is dependent upon organism-environment interactions that involve moral conflict.

Kohlberg has defined six stages of moral development. They are as follows (Kohlberg and Turiel, 1971):

A. *The Preconventional Child* considers labels of good or bad in terms of their physical consequences (punishment, reward) or in terms of the physical powers of those who establish the rules and apply the labels.
   Stage 1: Punishment and obedience orientation. The physical consequences of an action determine its goodness or badness, regardless of the human meaning or value of these consequences. Avoidance of punishment and unquestioning obedience are valued in their own right.
   Stage 2: Instrumental relativist orientation. Right action consists of that which instrumentally satisfies one's own needs and occasionally the needs of others.
B. *The Conventional Level* refers to conformism. Maintaining the expectations and rules of the individual's family, group, or nation is considered as valuable in its own right.
   Stage 3: Interpersonal concordance (good boy-nice girl) orientation. Good is that which pleases or helps others and is approved by them. Discord is avoided.
   Stage 4: Orientation toward authority ("law and order").

Obedience of authority, fixed rules for their own sake and for the maintenance of the status quo for the purpose of social order.

C. *The Postconventional Level* is characterized by a major thrust toward autonomous moral principles that have universal validity and application apart from the personal or legal authority of the groups who hold them and apart from the individual's personal identification with those persons or groups.

Stage 5: Social contract-orientation. Proper conduct tends to be defined in terms of general rights and standards that have been agreed upon by the whole society. There is a clear awareness of the variety of personal values and a corresponding emphasis upon procedural rules for reaching consensus. Emphasis is on the rule of laws, not men. This is the official morality of democratic nations.

Stage 6: Universal ethical principle orientation. Right is defined as a decision of conscience in accord with self-chosen ethical principles appealing to logical comprehensiveness, universality, and consistency. These principles are abstract and ethical (the Golden Rule) and not concrete moral rules. At heart, these are principles of justice, or the reciprocity and quality of human rights, and of respect for the dignity of humankind (pp. 415-416).

With a notion of stage similar to Piaget's, Kohlberg contends: (1) that these are stages of structure, not content; (2) that they form an invariant sequence in which attainment of an advanced stage is dependent on the attainment of each preceding stage; (3) that rate of progression through the stages is an individual variable; and (4) that an individual may be transitional between two adjoining stages—an indication of structural disequilibrium.

The claim for stages of moral development indicates, as is the case for cognitive development, that each new stage does not simply replace or extend the previous stage, but there is an accommodation (restructuring) to a more integrative method of moral judgment. Experimental evidence for this claim has been supplied by Rest, Turiel, and Kohlberg (1967) and Turiel (1966). Turiel found that movement to a moral stage different from that already in operation is always to the next highest level, thus supporting the claim for an invariant sequence. Further, when provided a choice, subjects preferred their own level or the next highest level and tended to resist reversion to a lower level of moral reasoning. Rest found that statements at stages above their subject's own are more difficult for subjects to understand, even though they may express a verbal preference for this reasoning. Kohlberg and Kramer (1969) have also provided cross-cultural information supportive to the claim for universality of sequence. These results imply that moral development is not simply a matter of learning the verbal rules of an individual culture. However, as with the cognitive studies, the data do support difference in the rate of development. For example, in preliterate or tribal groups, postconventional moral judgments appear to be absent or not fully developed.

To examine the relationship between moral judgment and moral behavior, Kohlberg (1966) has studied the incidence of cheating in preconventional, conventional, and postconventional individuals, following traditional admonitions against cheating. Not only was there a decline in the percentage of the postconventional individuals who cheated, but there was also more justification against cheating, based on principles of trust, fairness, and social agreement. This supports Kohlberg's contention that moral judgments, as measured by his testing procedures, are good predictors of moral behavior and that moral judgment is a necessary, but not sufficient, condition for moral behavior. Just as a new learning situation may cause an individual to try more familiar, but inadequate, thought processes, Kohlberg stipulates that emotional considerations may affect moral behavior even though adequate moral judgments are available.

Implications for Education
Despite the generalized time frames associated with the stages of cognitive development (seven to eleven years of age for concrete operations and eleven to fifteen years of age for formal operations [Inhelder and Piaget, 1958]), recent studies provide repeated evidence that a large proportion of graduating high school and college students lack the ability for formal thought. Studies by Friot (1970), Lawson, Nordland, and Devito (1974), and McKinnon (1970) indicate that on the average 50 percent of these populations are still at the concrete-operational level. Further studies by Karplus and Karplus (1970) and Kohlberg and Gilligan (1971) found only 50–65 percent of adult popula-

tions (twenty-one to fifty years of age) operating at the level of abstract thought. These data indicate that we are dealing with neither a strictly maturational nor a learning parameter when addressing the question of how these structures develop unless we hedge on the claim for the universality of their development by referring to inborn cognitive difference to explain these variations from the expected. Since developmentalists hold to the idea that mental operations arise from a self-regulated process in which the individual activity takes part in the solution of self-chosen problems that arise from his/her interaction with a complex environment (Lawson, 1979), we may ask the question: Do pedagogical techniques based on this paradigm achieve success?

To this question a qualified "Yes" answer must be given. The first qualification is due to the nature of the most successful studies. These studies employ an experimental design of one-to-one confrontation (subject-experimenter) using problems that have a noncontextual base (are not related to any specific content or subject matter). Positive results for both conservatory (Brainerd and Allen, 1971) and formal-operational reasoning (Lawson and Wollman, 1976) have been achieved. However, the increase for conservatory induction was only transferable to novel materials; that is, induced conservation did not facilitate acquisition or conservation of other quantities (nonspecific transfer). Further, transition to the formal-operational schemata was more pronounced for individuals in the transitional phase between concrete and formal reasoning. Studies using a contextual design (Rastovac, 1975; Walker, Mertens, and Hendrix, 1979) first analyzed the content according to necessary cognitive schemata, then designed instructional strategies to facilitate increased performance on questions requiring this development. In both cases positive results were achieved for those students in the transitional phase of development. Therefore, if learning paradigms are to be successful in promoting both increased performance on content requiring cognitive operations and cognitive development, these factors must be kept in mind: (1) the level of cognitive operation possessed by the student; (2) the cognitive operations required to understand the material; (3) the problems that can be presented concerning the material so as to move away from didactic instruction; and (4) the amount of time that should be allowed for the solution of the problem.

Kohlberg's approach to increasing the levels of moral judgment and behavior is also cognitive in nature. His approach combines value analysis and value clarification. He suggests the presentation of hypothetical moral dilemmas that will cause students to analyze the situations for possible solution and moral alternatives by class discussion. As the differences in analysis and resolution develop, Kohlberg feels that progress to the next highest level is likely to occur if the preferred resolution is at a stage that is one level above the student's spontaneous stage level, thus expanding upon and then consolidating a view compatible with the student's own development (Forisha and Forisha, 1976). Empirical support for this methodology has been reported by Blatt (1971) for the transition between stage 3 and stage 4. In this study group discussions were conducted, with the teacher supporting and clarifying arguments of students at the predominant level (stage 3). When these arguments seemed understood, a new problem was introduced and the teacher challenged the stage previously supported, while supporting arguments one stage higher (stage 4). Such procedures resulted in developmental change for 10 percent of the students.

The obvious question at this point is, "Can such practices be put into effect on a large scale, and will the results be worth the expenditure of time and energy?" Since the answer to this question is related to personal judgments on the adequacy of the individual theories presented in this paper, I can only offer the suggestion to examine the available literature further and to experiment on an individual basis.

A simple beginning point could be the examination of either the Piagetian tasks that analyze cognitive structure or Kohlberg's standardized procedure for moral-development assessment. The net result in most instances is a better understanding of one's own structure and the problems associated with trying to answer the question of structure genesis. This simple beginning, hopefully, will be beneficial to the continued cognitive and moral development of the students with whom we interact.

References

Ausubel, D. P. *The Psychology of Meaningful Verbal Learning.* New York: Grune & Stratton, 1963.

Blatt, M. "The Effects of Classroom Discussion upon Children's Level of Moral Judgement." In *Present Research in Moral Development,* edited by L. Kohlberg and E. Turiel. New York: Holt, Rinehart & Winston, 1971.

Bloom, B. S. "Learning for Mastery." *UCLA Evaluation Comment* 1 (1968):1-12.

Brainerd, C. "The Development of Proportionality Schema in Children and Adolescents." *Developmental Psychology* 5 (1971):469-76.

Elkind, D. "Children's Discovery of the Conservation of Mass, Weight and Volume: Piaget Replication Study II." *The Journal of Genetic Psychology* 98 (1961):219-27.

Forisha, B. E., and Forisha, B. E. *Moral Development and Education.* Lincoln, Neb.: Professional Educators Publications, 1976.

Friot, F. E. "The Relationship Between an Inquiry Teaching Approach and Intellectual Development." Unpublished Ph.D. dissertation, University of Oklahoma, 1970.

Gagne, R. M. *The Conditions of Learning.* New York: Holt, Rinehart & Winston, 1970.

Goldschmid, M. "Different Types of Conservation and Their Relation to Age, Sex, IQ, MA and Vocabulary." *Child Development* 38 (1967): 1229-46.

Inhelder, B., and Piaget, J. *The Growth of Logical Thinking from Childhood to Adolescence.* New York: Basic Books, 1958.

Kohlberg, L. "Moral Education in the Schools: A Developmental View." *The School Review* 74 (1966):1-20.

————. "Stages of Moral Development as a Basis for Moral Education." In *Moral Education: Interdisciplinary Approaches,* edited by C. Beck, B. Crittendon, and E. V. Sullivan. Toronto: University of Toronto Press, 1971.

Kohlberg, L., and Gilligan, C. "The Adolescent as a Philosopher: The Discovery of the Self in a Postconventional World." In *12-16: Early Adolescence,* edited by J. Kagan and R. Coles. New York: Norton, 1972.

Kohlberg, L., and Kramer, R. "Continuities and Discontinuities in Childhood and Adult Moral Behavior." *Human Development* 12 (1969): 93-120.

Kohlberg, L., and Mayer, R. "Development as the Aim of Education." *Harvard Educational Review* 42 (1972):449-96.

Kohlberg, L., and Turiel, E. "Moral Development and Moral Education." In *Psychology and Educational Practice,* edited by G. S. Lesser. Glenview, Ill.: Scott, Foresman, 1971.

Lawson, A. E. "Relationships between Concrete and Formal Operational Science Subject Matter and the Intellectual Level of the Learner." Unpublished Ph.D. dissertation, University of Oklahoma, 1973.

————. "The Developmental Learning Paradigm." *Journal of Research in Science Teaching* 16 (1979):501-16.

Lawson, A. E., Nordland, F., and Devito, A. "Piagetian Formal Operational Tasks: A Crossover Study of Learning Effect and Reliability." *Science Education* 58 (1974):267–76.

Lawson, A. E., and Wollman, W. "Encouraging the Transition from Concrete to Formal Cognitive Functioning–An Experiment." *Journal of Research in Science Teaching* 13 (1976):413–30.

McKinnon, J. W. "The Influence of a College Inquiry-Centered Course in Science on Student Entry into the Formal Operational Stage." Unpublished Ph.D. dissertation, University of Oklahoma, 1970.

Phillips, J. L. *The Origins of Intellect: Piaget's Theory.* San Francisco: Freeman, 1969.

Piaget, J. "Development and Learning." *Journal of Research in Science Teaching* 3 (1964):176–86.

———. *Structuralism.* Edited and translated by C. Maschler. New York: Basic Books, 1970.

Piaget, J., and Inhelder, B. *Le développement des quantités chez l'enfant.* Paris: Delachaux and Niestle, 1940.

———. *The Psychology of the Child.* New York: Basic Books, 1960.

Rastovac, J. "An Investigation of the Relationship Between a Mastery Learning Strategy and the Cognitive Level of High School Students." Unpublished Ph.D. dissertation, Purdue University, 1975.

Rest, J., Turiel, E., and Kohlberg, L. "Level of Moral Development." *Journal of Personality* 37 (1967):224–45.

Turiel, E. "An Experimental Test of the Sequentiality of Developmental Stages in the Child's Moral Judgment." *Journal of Personality and Social Psychology* 3 (1966):611–18.

Walker, R. A., Mertens, T., and Hendrix, J. "Formal Operational Reasoning Patterns and Scholastic Achievement in Genetics." *Journal of College Science Teaching* 8 (1979):156–58.

Dr. Werhane: We shall now hear from the three panelists. Our first panelist today is Maureen Fuechtmann, Director of University Ministry on the Lake Shore Campus for the past four years. She is a graduate of Youngstown State University. She has two M.A. degrees, one in theology and one in psychological counseling, as well as wide teaching and counseling experience.

Our second panelist is Dr. Thomas Wren, Associate Professor of Philosophy, who has been here since 1968. He graduated from St. Mary's College. He also has three master's degrees, one in education, one in English, and one in philosophy, and a Ph.D. from Northwestern in philosophy. He is the author of a book on ethical theories, *Agency and*

Urgency; he has published a number of articles on ethics; and he has a forthcoming book on the structure of moral motivation.

The third panelist is Father Bert Akers, Associate Professor of Communication Arts, at Loyola since 1978. A member of the Society of Jesus, Father Akers is a graduate of St. Louis University and holds a Ph.D. from Woodstock College. He was chairman of the Department of Theology at the University of Scranton. He has been production director of the Sacred Heart radio and television programming for eight years, and he is nationally known in the field of religious broadcasting and religious communication.

We shall first hear from Ms. Fuechtmann.

Ms. Fuechtmann: While acknowledging the enormous influence of the work on Kohlberg and Piaget and while being thoroughly convinced that we, as educators, must take their work seriously, I will limit my remarks today to some questions that are raised for me by Kohlberg's theory.

It could appear that Kohlberg's theory, from today's presentation and I think in his writing as well, is like a road that goes one way—from cognitive development to moral development. Kohlberg describes his model as interactionist: that is, it includes the role of someone (a teacher, a researcher, a psychologist) who promotes the restructuring of the subject's experience. I'm not sure that the model is clearly interactive. The direction seems to move from cognitive to moral development. The actual situation, it seems to me, is more complex. It is more like a two-way street between cognitive and moral development. In the real world, cognitive development may happen as a response to a lived moral situation. It's important to note that Kohlberg uses as a teaching strategy to advance cognitive development the exercise of living through hypothetical moral dilemmas. My suggestion is that in the real order we have moral dilemmas that have to be dealt with, solved, lived out. And the need to come to a solution of these moral dilemmas may push the individual in the direction of cognitive development. This indicates to me that the interaction between cognitive and moral development may be more of a two-way street than a one-way road.

My second difficulty is that Kohlberg's road may be too narrow. Kohlberg and his associates have been convinced that the stage system can operate as an instrument of moral education. The accuracy and techniques for such claims must be judged by continuing research, but it seems plausible that broadening the moral development perspectives could increase the possibility of advancement to the next stage. Kohlberg has been criticized repeatedly for being particularly weak on the affective side of morality. In response to this, Paul Philibert, O.P., in a recent article in *Horizons* entitled "Conscience: Developmental Perspectives . . ." discusses his rediscovering in some early work of Carl Rogers a stage structure that has many similarities to Kohlberg's but is articulated entirely in terms of the subject's developing self-appreciation and personal freedom. It is possible, Philibert contends, that the coupling of an affective behavioral continuum with Kohlberg's moral-reasoning continuum would provide a more balanced approach to understanding moral development. Kohlberg holds that cognitive development is a necessary but an insufficient condition for moral reasoning. If I were to stick with my road metaphor, I would call to mind the image of a limited-access road. Kohlberg's entire moral structure rests upon a conception of morality and of conscience that is concerned with the universal prescriptive system of resolving claims of distributive justice. Justice is his category. But the world of moral education is larger than the matter of justice. Critics of this stance believe that it allows central moral issues to pass completely through the structural sieve. Here again, I see the need of other models of development that include the affective dimension to complement the Kohlbergian perspective. In his system there is no room for concepts such as character, love, and courage. Also, while it is apparent that Kohlberg never intended to produce a Christian ethical theory, it is difficult to place fundamental dynamics for moral development from the Christian perspective such as vocation, movement of the Spirit, or invitation to grace and faith anywhere in his schema. I think I would conclude that, as Kohlberg says that cognitive development is a necessary but an insufficient condition for moral reasoning, Kohlberg's contributions have been an undeniably important but insufficient basis for moral education.

The paper that we have listened to explores cognitive and moral development and provides a place where we can stand together in an academic-pluralistic environment with some common ground to ask further questions, to probe deeper into the ramifications of our task as educators. Kohlberg's notion is that in a developmental definition of educational aims there is required both the method of philosophy or ethics and the method of psychology or science. This implies that the understanding of logical and ethical principles is a central aim of education. Is there—should there be, therefore —an ethics course that is required for undergraduates here? Should a logic course be required? Or should ethics and logic, like writing, although they can be taught in formal courses, be pervasive in the kind of educational system we are about? And if Kohlberg and Piaget are not enough, then how can we, as educators, be part of the process that expands their vision?

Dr. Werhane: Thank you. Our second panelist is Dr. Thomas Wren.

Dr. Wren: I feel that some of my thunder has been stolen by the last commentator's objections to Kohlberg's intellectualism. If her role was that of devil's advocate, then I suppose mine is something like that of a supplemental witness. At any rate, I'd like to begin with a reminder of the tremendous implications that go into conceiving of morality as a developmental process at all, never mind whether the developmental process is cognitively or affectively conceived. Moral developmental theories are by no means the only sorts of moral psychology, either the technical moral psychology that is conceived in psychological journals or the nontechnical moral psychology that has been conceived over the years as part of our Western heritage. Only recently have people stopped assuming that conscience is inborn in children, an assumption that generally led people to judge children's misbehaviors extremely harshly. In that view, the inscrutable intuitions of conscience were thought to provide criteria for selecting out one motivational and normative system as *the* moral one for every age group, and God help any child who deviated from the course of righteousness.

The polar opposite of this view, which is equally nondevelopmental, is that of the various moral psychologies that are conceived as corollaries of modern social learning theory. These eschew both the innate-conscience idea and that of foreordained patterns of moral development, stressing instead the necessity in moral education for adult intervention on behalf of whatever culturally shared norms are presently in effect. Now this approach, reminiscent as it is of the seventeenth-century notion of the mind as a *tabula rasa*—a blank slate—conceives of morality entirely in terms of socially specified acts and avoidances whose only ethical validity is their having been approved in a social consensus. Beyond that rather vague definition, this view contains no overall conception of morality and no specifically moral norms (as distinct from, say, matters of taste). Instead of universal moral categories, there are only general psychological tendencies, such as the tendency of a child or adult learner to take his cues from others by way of modeling, reinforcement, or whatever. This is a considerably diminished version of that fundamental concern which in this symposium and elsewhere we have been calling morality.

And so moral development is only one of the theories of morality or moral learning. My own sympathies are with the developmental line, but I differ from Professor Rastovac in that I hold a considerably less cognitively biased theory of moral development. I am not going to make any positive case here for an affectively biased theory, however, though you can imagine from Ms. Fuechtmann's comments what such a theory would include. I would just like to share some of the misgivings I have about the highly logical character of moral development as it was presented in the preceding paper.

First of all, speaking directly of the Kohlbergian theory, I should announce that many philosophers have already gone on record as balking at the normative premises that Kohlberg, Piaget, and other so-called cognitive-developmentalists have identified with the highest stage of moral development. I think it might not be a bad idea if I were just to remind you what Kohlberg's six stages of moral judgment are. There are three principal divisions: preconventional, conventional, and postconventional. "Postconventional" means, most briefly, that you think for yourself. "Preconventional" means that you have not yet been socialized. "Conventional" means the part in between, which is where most adults are. Each of these three divisions has two subdivisions or stages, so that we have a total of six stages. Stage 1 is called heteronomous morality; the orientation is strictly in terms of punishment and obedience. Stage 2, also presocial, is individualism that has a kind of incipient social character to it; it's a you-scratch-my-back-I'll-scratch-yours sort of cooperation. Stage 3, which is the first of the truly socialized stages, is conformity to expectations within interpersonal relationships such as are found in the family. Stage 4, which is the higher of the two conventional stages, is a system-maintaining morality in which, say, the child asks, "What is good for the whole family?" rather than "What does my mother want me to do? What does my brother want me to do?" With stage 5 we emerge into postconventional or "principled" thinking. This is described by Kohlberg in various ways, but the main ideas are those of utilitarianism and social-contract theory (an alliance of theories that many philosophers, including myself, find troublesome on both historical and formal grounds). Stage 6 goes beyond the principles of utilitarianism and social-contract theory to an even higher, more elegant form of principled thinking—that of universal ethical principles. The most familiar expression of stage 6 is our Bill of Rights, which can be boiled down to the idea of impartial fair play.

Now many philosophers are uneasy about the fact that Kohlberg, who announces very explicitly that he is working not with specific contents but only with modes of reasoning, seems to have smuggled into the description of the highest and methodologically most important stage a set of values that are eminently culture bound—that is, specific contents rather than general forms of moral reasoning. I hope that distinction is clear, since, although it's crucial, I really don't have time to develop it here. Suffice it to say that the cognitive-developmentalist professes to be interested only in the *arguments* a moral reasoner uses to get to moral conclusions, whatever those conclusions may be, and not in the moral *values* specific to them. Philosophers tend to be a querulous group, and they are particularly upset by the fact that Kohlberg starts off indicating he will not tie his theory up with any one set of moral norms but only with the progressively sophisticated modes of reasoning toward norms of any sort, and then the highest level of moral reasoning turns out to be, lo! a set of moral norms. This seems to be the problem that is most discussed in the philosophical literature about Kohlberg; I don't propose to resolve it here, but I would like to alert you to it.

There are a lot of other problems, such as: Why should we call the earlier stages "moral" systems at all? But the problem that intrigues me the most, and the one with which I shall conclude, is this. It seems inevitable that you would have as the end stage of any cognitive-developmental theory— be it of moral judgment, science learning, mathematics learning, or whatever skill is in question—a skill or psychological capacity that is very, very structured. I say this because cognitive-developmentalism is essentially an inquiry into the acquisition and use of *rules*. Hence the final stage of moral development is one in which, to echo Kohlberg's philosophical patron Immanuel Kant, the agent acts as though he or she were legislating universal principles of conduct, applicable to all persons and forming an integral legislative system. This is certainly one way to think of morality. But it's by no means self-evident that the very highest mode of morality has to be a highly structured and rule-governed form of life. It could be that the most beautiful, elegant, and advanced form of moral living is closer to artistic improvisation, in which one just "wings it." Maybe we should enshrine intuitions rather than principled thinking at the final stage. I say "maybe" because the debate on this issue is still very much in full swing. Insofar as Professor Rastovac, Kohlberg, Piaget, and other advocates of the cognitive-developmental view presuppose the outcome of that debate, they do so at their own risk.

Dr. Werhane: Thank you. The third panelist is Father Akers.

Father Akers: Human things are so passing. In an age that could be described as early Bo Derek, the only thing to be is a 10. But it was not so long ago that the magic number was 6. That was the time when facilitators at Transactional Analysis meetings would say "I want all the 6s in that corner of the room." A needless directive if there ever was one, because 6s had ways of finding one another across the crowded room. It was the closet 3s and 4s who needed help.

So I came to Kohlberg late, after hearing a great many things about him over many years, in many discussions, in many disciplines. There were even times when the magic name of Kohlberg was used like a gavel rap to terminate further discussion. But in some ways I was fortunate: I came to Kohlberg late—but not breathless. And I found an interesting thing: As is so often the case, scholars who have become celebrities are not always doing what the public thinks they're doing. (They are not even always doing what *they* think they're doing.)

Certainly Professor Kohlberg, a man so eminent and who has contributed so much to this field, needs no defense. It may be we who need a defense, a caution or two about the limitations in his system and the all-but-inevitable problem of seeing an effective methodology become so reified that the "stages of development" become as firm as a flight of steps, and an analysis become an ethical imperative and even a program for social or educational reform.

Surely a developmental approach to the question of ethics is a most welcome contribution. But is it, in its essentials, new? Or is it not rather a healthy and needed reaction to a very atrophied ethical theory (reflecting a nonhistorical notion of "human nature" and a somewhat mystical conception of "conscience" as infused and universal, enabling those of good will to leave the bassinet with something rather like a High Anglican scale of values)—a regression, really, and not at all representative of the great insights and wisdom of Western ethical thought?

That achievement—and a highly "developmental" approach to ethics—finds much better expression in the great Latin phrase *recta ratio agendorum*: right thinking about conduct, right thinking about decisions for action—a dynamic process for ethical decision that goes back from the Scholastics through the Stoics through Aristotle and is found in a question posed with exquisite clarity and haunting poignancy at the beginning of Plato's *Meno*: "Can you tell me, O Socrates, whether virtue is acquired by teaching or by practice, or, if neither by teaching nor practice, then whether it comes to man by nature or in what other way?" One can only hope that it is not this great tradition, which not only allows for but demands the full involvement and development of the *person,* that Kohlberg treats somewhat condescendingly and scornfully describes as that "bag of virtues." Or is it not rather that tradition's stuffed remains, the perennial and disastrous efforts of the "manualists" to reduce the richness, the untidiness, the very swoop and glide, the creativity and high drama of the moral life to a compendium of rules for safe conduct?

Still, we need to accept the challenge Kohlberg's system offers us and question the limitations in our own. What have been the inadequacies in our own approach to ethical development that have made his approach so appealing? In returning to the riches of our own tradition, we do not need in any way to negate his valuable contributions but to complement them, setting them within the older but, I believe, broader framework.

A final suggestion. We are heirs not only to a philosophical tradition but to the Judeo-Christian religious tradition. By what mandate, I wonder, must we yield serious ethical discussion to the positivists and the naturalists? The Judeo-Christian tradition has (granting all its sinful failures) managed to call forth the highest ethical and moral responses human beings are capable of. Even as a "wisdom" (apart from being a revealed Faith), this tradition has a great deal to say about such topics (in Kohlberg's categories) as punishment, obedience, hedonism, about good-boy/nice-girl morality, about authority, loyalty, human rights, and certainly about conscience—all this, though Christianity is not primarily about ethics or morality. Christianity is not essentially a creed—let alone a code. It is not first of all *about* anything. It is about Someone. It is absolutely personal, thoroughly developmental. It demands as a matter of course total commitment, total self-transcendence. We don't live it very well—but that is what it is.

Too bad more of our ethicists don't realize that the Christian tradition is there. Kohlberg himself was looking. In his later writings he was groping towards a stage 7. He recognized that to have any ethics, you have to have a kind of total ethics. You have to face the ultimate questions: Why should I be just? Why should I be just in an unjust world?

Why should I live? What is the meaning of life? The Christian answer is given not in terms of justice only but of love.

Dr. Werhane: We will now give Dr. Rastovac an opportunity to comment on the remarks of the three panelists.

Dr. Rastovac: First of all, in relation to the question, "Is the interaction between cognitive and moral development a one-way or a two-way street?" I think there is the possibility that people are misinterpreting Piaget and Kohlberg. First of all, Kohlberg does not say that cognitive development is a sufficient condition for moral development or that it necessarily leads into moral development. He says that it is a necessary condition for moral judgment.

As an example, let me read the following passage. This will illustrate the difference between an individual at the concrete-operational stage and an individual making the transition to formal or abstract thought. Here is the problem first posed to the concrete individual: "What does the Golden Rule tell you to do if someone comes up to you on the street and hits you?" This person might say, "Hit him back. Do to others as they do unto you." But the reversal of the reciprocal is demanded, and this is what you'll see in the development of the transitional phase, or a slight movement into formal operations: "Well, for the Golden Rule, you have to like dream that your mind leaves your body and goes into the other person and it comes back into you and you see it like he does and you act the way you saw it from there."

Now how many ways can you see it from there? I don't know. How large is the cognitive structure? I don't think that the idea of a two-way street is ruled out. The concept of reversibility is central to both theories; therefore, your moral stage can present a problem that can lead to cognitive development because the environment includes not only things external to you but also what you have internalized through that development. The inner action is not simply bouncing off things external. Further, there's nothing wrong with the idea of broadening a moral base so that it may lead to moral development. Both Piaget and Kohlberg talk about horizontal décalage as an influential factor in both cognitive and moral development.

As for the definition of *stage,* one thing should be kept in mind. Structure is the important thing, not the formalization that we develop when we are trying to express what the structure is. It is very difficult even to explain or understand your own structure. You have to develop some kind of formalism. Mathematical formalism for Piaget is probably easiest. I'm not that familiar with Kohlberg's formalism, but they are both talking about the structure, not the formalization of the structure. And that structure is not static, it is dynamic. It is the formalization that gives the impression that the structure is static.

Also, I think stage 7 has been slightly misinterpreted. I think it is very close to what's referred to as a cosmic-unity stage. How does that fit into a religious perspective? From this point of view, your concept of God is no longer the same as it was when you were in the preconventional or postconventional stage. This does not imply that religion hasn't any input, or that there is not a God. Difficulties arise when individuals at different stages of development attempt to express their notions of God to each other. It becomes a problem of communication, not belief.

Member of the audience: I think you indicated just now that cognitive development is necessary for moral judgment but not for moral development. I'm not sure.

Dr. Rastovac: It's a necessary condition for moral judgment, but it's not sufficient. While you may be able to think in a logical manner, you don't necessarily have to act morally on a conventional (stage 4) or postconventional level.

Member of the audience: Do any members of the panel want to answer this question: What is the relation between moral judgment and behavior?

Dr. Wren: Do I *want* to answer that? I want very much to answer it. The problem is, I'm not sure I can, but I'll try. I certainly think it's terribly important to the integrity of what Kohlberg and the other people, including Rastovac, are trying to do, that there be a gap between one's ability to judge and one's actual performance. Otherwise we would have the totally bizarre prospect of a psychology claiming that it could, by certain teaching techniques alone, guarantee moral conduct, so that moral evil would be extinguished by sheer pedagogical virtuosity. I don't know anyone who has ever thought he or she was *that* good as a teacher! Kohlberg, in his own attempts to deal with this question, suddenly starts using a lot of very affective terms, terms like "self-esteem" and "role models," figuring, I suppose, that these motivational concepts will take up the slack between the cognitive judgment that this is what one ought to do and the actual practical judgment or decision: "This is what I shall do." Perhaps we ought to distinguish two interwoven but different strands of moral education: that of teaching people what they ought to do, which, as all teachers know, entails a whole battery of motivational techniques, and that of getting people to do what they have learned, which would entail another quite different motivational program. But there is certainly an overlap between the two sorts of motivation, at least at the higher levels of development. It seems to me that if a person is morally mature, there ought to be some intrinsic appeal attached to the very lucidity of the moral principles that have been discovered. Without trying to say where this appeal comes from (some philosophers suppose it to be produced by a moral sense), I certainly wouldn't want it to get lost sight of.

Another point, please. One of the problems I glided past a moment ago is Kohlberg's method of getting his subjects to grapple with hypothetical moral dilemmas. But most moral agents don't spend much of their time sorting out dilemmas. The dilemma is the *unusual* moment in a moral life, not the usual one. Since Kohlberg has taken this highly unusual phenomenon and built his whole analysis of moral living around it, it is possible that any patterns he discovers will be irrelevant to most of the population of the moral domain.

Father Robert Bireley, S.J.: I would like to ask the panelists whether the following points fit into their theory or not. The first is that one function of the liberal arts is to confront the students with the value systems of other times and periods of history and, in doing this, to make them become more aware of their own value systems, reflect on them, and as a result grow. I would like to have that related to the theory you have presented. Secondly, it seems to me that one function of history (I teach history) is to awaken the students to different moral problems in the world today. As I understand it, many moral theorists would say that initially our moral horizons are limited to our own immediate family and friends, and that we later come to the point where we see community issues in moral terms. Many people, perhaps, never arrive at the point where they think morally about issues beyond their own community. History, then, points out broader moral issues just by giving information, not necessarily telling people or hinting to them what they ought to do about these moral issues. This it does, for example, when it looks at the situation in many underdeveloped countries and points up the maldistribution of wealth in the world. Is this also not an element in the development of moral life? Thirdly, the study of history—as well as that of literature and other liberal subjects, for that matter—awakens a person to the complexity of issues—the causes of inflation, for example, or the responsibility for the Reformation. These are terribly complex issues, where there is never a question of "the good guys versus the bad guys." There is good and bad on both sides. Now an awareness of this complexity, it seems to me, is again an element in the development of one's moral thinking. Among other things, it protects us against the temptation to seek simple solutions or, worse, scapegoats. This is another manner in which the liberal arts contribute to the development of moral attitudes. I wonder whether Dr. Rastovac or the panelists would relate that to their theories, or perhaps I am being too practical at this point.

Dr. Rastovac: I'd like to try. Let me borrow something from the social area. By awareness you could mean (and I'm not saying this is what you would say) an understanding that social Darwinism is unjustified. But I'd have very serious questions about making that statement in a course in evolution. It demands theoretical reasoning ability to understand that Darwin's theory is based on a materialistic philosophy and that it is a theory and not a natural law. It cannot be used to justify interpretations and decisions of cultural evolution. I doubt that my just pointing that out to the students is going to make any major changes in their thought processes. However, I have a student who is trying to formulate as problems for class discussion two criminal cases where the maximum penalty would be the death penalty, followed in severity by decreasing prison sentences. The major difference between the cases, and this goes back to a theory on criminal behavior by Lombroso, is that one individual will be described as a "natural-born psychopath" with a long history of violent criminal behavior, while the other is a victim of circumstances. The two cases will be randomly distributed to her fellow students in her criminal justice class. They are to function as judges, that is, select the penalty and describe their reasons. Is criminality an inherited characteristic? Is it a natural condition for some individuals? How could you defend a viewpoint like that? I believe that pondering questions like these, after examining the responses, will have more influence on development than simple awareness that there is a problem. I believe awareness is best facilitated and enhanced by activity.

Dr. Wren: One of the features of both Kohlberg's and Piaget's notions of the cognitive stages is the fact that the higher stage involves the ability to take a point of view on the lower stage. For instance, the morally developed stage 4 child takes the point of view on the whole set of one-on-one relationships that are the stuff of a stage 3 child's thought process. That is, a typical stage 3 conflict would be one between the child's obligations to the mother and obligations to a brother or sister. The stage 3 child is capable of appreciating those two obligations as embodying terribly relevant roles (peer, son, or daughter) but doesn't connect them to each other. The stage 4 child, who, as I said, takes a point of view on those relationships, sees the family as a holistic system consisting in a *network of relationships.* To put my point most generally, the relative excellence of any stage lies in its ability to take a unified and unifying perspective on the diverse processes and objects of the lower stage, as an ophthalmologist enjoys a perspective on visual processes and perspectives not available to those of us who use our eyes but never look at our eyes. Now it seems to me that this way of conceiving cognitive development—as the ability to take a perspective on a plurality of other perspectives—is echoed in the first remark you made, Father Bireley, to the effect that a person who is in the grip of a culture doesn't take a perspective on that culture. The person may have some scattered information about it, as well as about other cultures, but doesn't see any of them as true cultural systems. A liberal arts education would presumably stimulate this person's cognitive development to the point or level of being able to take a perspective on cultural perspectives (including one's own). Would that new perspective itself be a cultural system, liable to revision from a still higher point of view? Probably. But this need not be the monotonously nondevelopmental story about great fleas having lesser fleas that bite 'em, ad infinitum. On the contrary, I think that the cognitive-developmental model of increasingly better, albeit parasitic, perspectives is most apt to the liberal-arts ideal and could be worked out quite elegantly to deal with that first, to me very interesting, remark you made. Does that make any sense? I hope it does, since I think one of the marvelous things in liberal arts is that it enables one to transcend one's historical limits by taking a perspective on them.

Dr. Werhane: We have had a very exciting afternoon. We have experienced a very general approach to ethics with Father Harvanek's discussion of the concept of the person. Following this, John Rastovac has presented a more specific analysis of ethical education. Following the theory of Lawrence Kohlberg, Rastovac argues that education in moral development is necessary for moral decision making to take place. Ethical education begins with the introduction of cognitive procedural operations, which induce, in progressive stages, moral awareness and facilitate the making of moral judgments, which become more sophisticated and universal in nature at each stage of the ethical learning process. And Rastovac suggests that, if one does not progress through stages of moral development, one's moral awareness and hence one's moral judgment making remain always at a very elementary level. Rastovac places the burden of the possibility of ethical education squarely on the educator. He is not suggesting that one teach values, but he argues that without the introduction, in stages, of moral development into the educational process, ethical education and hence the teaching of values is impossible.

As the commentators have aptly pointed out, the development of moral awareness and the capacity to make universal moral judgments sets the stage for, but is not identified with, moral education. Moral development is, at best, a necessary but not a sufficient condition for moral education. Maureen Fuechtmann, in her comments, suggests that Kohlberg and Rastovac omit an analysis of the affective side of moral development, which is as important as cognition in moral education. Finally, Father Akers proposes that the ethical dimension of human life is not identified with the education of moral development as Kohlberg describes this process. He suggests that the last stage of moral development might entail a deep questioning of the process of morality, the making of moral judgments, and the justification of the moral life. This questioning process projects one beyond the cognitive and affective sides of human experience to a commitment to an ethic, perhaps a Christian ethic through the experience of love.

I now yield the floor to Father McMahon for his concluding remarks.

Father McMahon: My challenge is to tie up as much as we can. We started out this afternoon by talking about two concepts of the theory of ethics: basic theory on the one hand, and theory of ethical growth and development on the other hand. The approaches that the panelists presented were quite different from the traditional methods of talking about ethics in a Catholic university. The goals have not changed, but the methodologies and the approach have changed.

I would like to mention a number of points that the panels covered. First of all, ethics is still considered primarily as normative. Secondly, ethics includes more than knowledge and the cognitive aspect. Third, role models seem to be required in ethical development. Fourth, religious perspectives cannot be isolated from the ethical experience.

Fifthly, structure has some relationship to ethics in an ethical approach. Sixthly, in a Christian university justice is an important value that prepares the way to love and to wisdom. I'd like to end with a statement from Father Harvanek's paper: "Though the university indeed is distinct from the city, it is distinct not as one of two competing social groups, but as a part of the whole, and a very important, even essential, part. The university is one of the agents for the production of the city of man. If it is a Christian university, then it is also an agent for the development of the city of God."

PANEL 3
Seated: Mr. Patrick McGinty
and Ms. Marilyn Miller

Standing: Mr. Mark Lauer,
Mr. Michael O'Toole,
Ms. Margaret Kelly,
Ms. Magdalen Belickas,
Mr. Kevin Coley,
Mr. Terry Johnson
(from left to right)

PANEL 3

Moderator:
Mr. Patrick McGinty

Competition: Conflict or Cooperation
Ms. Marilyn Miller

Honesty and Academia
Ms. Margaret Kelly, Mr. Mark Lauer
Mr. Michael O'Toole, Ms. Magdalen Belickas

Persons-for-Others
Mr. Kevin Coley, Mr. Terry Johnson

Father Thomas McMahon, C.S.V.: During the first symposium, last Thursday, we discussed theoretical ethical concepts. Father Harvanek provided the basis for ethical decision making as he explored five different contrasts: value and moral value, knowledge and virtue, morality and religion, learning and the climate of learning, and university and city. Later, Dr. Rastovac pursued the concept of cognitive and moral development with an emphasis on two authors, Piaget and Kohlberg.

Last week we investigated the basic theory of ethics. This week we will apply the basic theory to specific issues. First, student presenters will cover the practical ethical problems they have experienced in their university education. Afterwards, faculty from the professional schools will discuss issues involved in the teaching of ethics. Before we go into this, I'd like to acknowledge two persons who have been deeply involved in both the planning and implementation of this symposium: one is Dr. James Barry, who was the prime mover, if you will; the other is Father Joseph Small, who put the practical details of these two days together.

The moderator for this panel is Mr. Patrick McGinty. A major in public accounting in the School of Business Administration, Pat is serving this year as a member of the Publications Board and as coeditor of our student literary magazine, *Cadence*. We are all grateful to him for the important role he has played in the development of this panel. Mr. Patrick McGinty.

Mr. Patrick McGinty: Thank you, Father. I think before we begin it would be appropriate to give you some background information on what you are going to be hearing. Last fall Dr. Barry called together student leaders from various organizations in the university and asked them this question: What values and ethical behaviors are important to students at Loyola? The students had to think about that for a minute. When they overcame the shock, they came up with several ideas. A committee was formed to evaluate what some of these ideas were, and a format for presenting these ideas was discussed. What you are going to hear today, then, is a result of that work. I do not think we have the answers to all the questions that were posed last week. I *do* think the student panel is a very exciting part of the symposium. It offers a flavoring of the different segments of the student community here at Loyola.

The first speaker, Marilyn Miller, holds a B.S. degree in medical technology from Marquette University and a master's degree in biology from Loyola; she is presently pursuing a doctorate in anatomy at Loyola.

The second presenter, Margaret Kelly, is a senior at Loyola and a political science major. She is also a member of the Lake Shore Student Government Association. The paper she is presenting has four authors: Margaret Kelly, Mark Lauer, Michael O'Toole, and Magdalen Belickas. Mark Lauer is a past winner of the President's Medallion, coordinated the Hunger Committee, and is a vice-president of Tri Beta. Michael

O'Toole, a senior biology major, is a Gonzaga Hall officer and a member of the Honors Program. Magdalen Belickas, also a senior biology major, is active with the *Phoenix* and in the Honors Program.

The third paper will be presented by Kevin Coley, a junior in the College of Arts and Sciences. He has been a Hunger Week coordinator for the last two years and is a member of the Academic Council and of the TKE fraternity. His coauthor, Terry Johnson, holds a B.S. degree in psychology from Loyola. He is presently pursuing a master's degree in pastoral studies here at Loyola and is very active in the student ministry program.

Our format is going to be a little bit different today. The students felt that, to create something very meaningful as a result of the symposium, there should be some type of interaction. What we would like to do is create a type of forum; after each presentation we encourage you to give us your questions, your ideas, and your positions and to interact with us on what has been said.

I should now like to present our first speaker, Marilyn Miller.

Competition: Conflict or Cooperation
Ms. Marilyn Miller

Albert Einstein once said, "For all, life is either a win or lose proposition, with the prize of survival going to the fittest." We come from a tradition that strongly supports individuality in the pursuit of success. Our aggressive attitude toward the process of attaining societal and personal goals permeates almost all the institutional organizations and forums in our culture. We practically take this approach for granted. What would be the result if we did not?

Darwin, in talking about the evolutionary process, stated that teleologically organisms are faced with a decision in an environment that is becoming ever more hostile to their existence. They must change or die. Most of us would choose the former option.

What does this mean in today's highly technological and merit-oriented society? It means, simply, competition—competition on all levels: personal, familial, professional, economic, political, and—the level discussed today—scholastic.

Within the academic community, there are strong efforts to achieve intellectual integrity and independence, emotional self-sufficiency and maturity. How these goals are achieved is a matter both for introspection and public forums like this one. The process is not self-evident. Academic competition is no less ruthless than the competition for natural resources, for this struggle involves our very self-image, our identity, and our sense of control over our environment. To achieve academic success, we are willing to take risks, perhaps even to do harm. As students, we may frequently feel that the ends are more important than the means: that the diploma is more important than what we came here to learn. Educators may often feel that we students are acting irresponsibly towards the contract we sign when we enter college. This contract is to learn, to understand, and to use our talents to the limits of our capability; to challenge ourselves, and to allow ourselves to change.

Some may believe that the humanistic values held by a Christian university are in conflict with Darwinian competition. Following Darwinian logic, we would throw the aged out into the cold and leave the blind, weak, and deaf unprotected and without guidance. If competition is to exist in academia, what form of it should prevail? At its worst, it is detrimental and counterproductive to the student, to peers, to the university, and to the educational process. In this more dangerous form, it poisons friendship, makes knowledge a secondary goal, and turns the mind from the happy pursuit of truths to envy and deceit. Alternatively, in its petty and misinformed condition, it engenders self-serving compromises between students and self-delusions about their capabilities. This type of competition is distastefully mediocre, unenlightened, and compromising. However, competition at its best may be a healthy aspect of the educational process, stimulating sound intellectual development among minds interested in the same goals.

Faced with the potential problems, how can the student come to live by the most positive aspects of competition? I believe it can be achieved by understanding against whom he or she is really competing. To me, ideally, students will find themselves to be their own keenest, yet most understanding, competitors. That is to say, we are our own best teachers. The mature and enthusiastic competitor must first be convinced of his or her own intellectual promise, look within, and challenge himself or herself.

The student body of this university arises from heterogeneous social, economic, cultural, religious, and parental origins. We are diverse in nature, amorphous in form, and embryonic in development. Upon admission to college, we are cast into a community whose standards we do not know, whose values we may not appreciate, but whose authority is absolute and pervasive. Herein lies a conflict: how can this multitude of personalities be assimilated into the university, with all of its institutional and ethical expectations, without discord and disagreement? How can students learn to succeed, how can they learn to achieve, without compromising their individuality?

We as students have a common goal: to reach upward for fulfillment and become competent in various academic areas. This task is to be achieved in an environment that is often stressful, and where there are often struggles for recognition. In a sense, personal competition is perceived as being comparative in nature, that is, "competence on a curve." This is a perversion that may set the stage for further errors in thinking. And, carrying this thinking further, since there are more students than there are "As," if we are to get our fair share of As, we are forced to compete. Some will have to settle for less than As. But with whom are we competing? With a system that is sensitive to comparative rather than competence-oriented learning? With our peers? Or with ourselves?

In the university setting, we soon learn that there are standards that our educators wish us to achieve. These standards are high, and we want them to be high so that we can strive for new spheres of experience. This is part of our contract with learning. Yet these standards extend beyond just grades. They deal with our potentials as human beings. Once we understand this, we may begin to understand what might be called the "academic imperative": to close the gap between where we are and where we ought to be. This imperative forces the emergent student to ask himself or herself, "Can I be trusted to act honorably when faced with pressures that I have never experienced or imagined? When I am faced with the possibility of personal failure and abandonment by the academic community, by my friends, or by my family? If I must succeed, at what price? At the price of my personal integrity?" When given a test of our knowledge, can we be trusted to respect the honor code? If one student sells out to get a good grade, is another likely to do the same? The person who is not honest is not willing to take a chance on himself or herself but would rather depend on others. If the professor is willing to leave the room during an examination, is it "every man for himself"? At its most base level, competition *is* "every man for himself"; and what does that give us? We find students so caught up in their misplaced goals that they lose the ability to laugh, to be reflective, and to enjoy these "good old days" that they will speak of in the future. These are students so intent upon achieving high grades that they may forfeit their physical and mental health for them. No title, no place in post-graduate education is worth a tortured or unhealthy mind. Suicides, nervous breakdowns, or deep depression over blighted hopes are the sour fruit of competition run amok for people who let the desire for success rule them and perish from it.

There is another type of contest among bibliophiles. This more petty form of competition is found in a peculiar environment. Some of the techniques used in this forum include downgrading fellow students to peers or professors to look better, asking others their test scores, and finding sneaky ways of ascertaining others' scores for ego reinforcement. Sometimes small groups of students participate in these activities; like commando squads, these "gunners" and "cutthroats" sit in the first few rows of the classroom with recording devices and pens in four hues so as not to miss one colorful word from the professor's mouth. Alternately, some equally irritating but less dedicated students who might be best referred to as "academic saboteurs" can be found in the back of the room chattering away, exercising their own form of competition. If they cannot compete with the cutthroats, they will at least prevent them from learning. Some intellectual dilettantes have been known to amass huge volumes of old exams and lab reports from the fraternities or sororities with the answers to hundreds of possible questions. They buy books entitled *How to Get Good Grades Without Really Trying,* or words to that effect. There are students who, with razor blades, cut pages out of books so that no one else can have an equal chance to study the material. This occurs particularly when they cannot permanently retire a book from circulation from the school's library. Some make great effort to analyze the professor: easy, hard, unpredictable, full of quirks, or boring. They go into examinations arrogantly predicting the professor's questions, grading approach, and attitudes, cutting as many corners as possible in their studying and having tried as many ways as possible to "beat the system." The best of the cutthroats feels very badly inside when, after all machinations, he or she does not earn the highest grade; the chatterers in the back do not really care, since they did not expect to do any better than just pass anyway. They are happy that they were able to stay awake during the class period. That was their achievement. This type of competition is not necessarily bad and may bring rewards to students who are not aware of where they are going, but is this the academic spirit to which we should aspire?

Now that we have observed the less savory aspects of educational competition, let us view what we may do to build a university as it more ideally could be: a place where students are concerned with the pursuit of knowledge and truth. We are at the university to gain, not to lose. What can we do to gain from competition? Despite the best efforts to build a good academic setting, there are still temptations. To the professors, I would say: Please do not make it more difficult for the honest student to remain honest. To the students, I would say: Follow your own interests and instincts, and you will inevitably do well. The best way to find your niche is to do things at which you are successful or things that make you happy, and not what someone tells you should be your aspirations, happiness, or strengths. There is no limitation to your potential, as long as you recognize what you can do with it. It is a hard-fought battle just to be you. Do not miss the you that you are capable of becoming. Dedicate yourself to the process of looking within to build on strengths that are yours. You must confront yourself with your own dreams and expectations. This is a personal encounter from which you should not escape. In the words of Fritz Perls, "You don't have to push the river; it flows by itself." If you allow yourself to flow with your talents, you will find a comfortable place among the multitude of personalities in this university and will be assimilated into it without dissent or disagreement. This is the solution to the conflict of how to succeed and achieve without compromising your individuality.

As in every Christian university, the first concern at Loyola should not be the academic field but the personal field: the individual's personal growth and worth. The primary goal of the university should be to make good people. In the competitive system it pays at times not to be good. What can be said to people who have turned away from academic honesty? The only solution to this dilemma is a fundamental commitment to the Self that does not tolerate the word "cheat" or "liar" to be associated with it. One's first duty in life is not to betray the Self. As Shakespeare so eloquently phrased it: "This above all: to thine own self be true, / And it must follow, as the night the day, / Thou canst not then be false to any man." To compete with yourself, to make the best Self possible, would make the temptation to take from another so that you can add to a false Self no temptation at all. The first challenge throughout life is to build a better Self, and that will brook no falsehood.

Competition with Self will help the student take pride in his or her achievements and will not tempt the student to take credit for the achievements of others. It will help the student to look with a realistic eye upon himself or herself in comparison with the more or less gifted student and to act in a fashion concordant with his or her own ability. It will be the student's encouragement to make a genuine contribution to the improvement of society. It is said that Einstein failed in grammar school, and yet he followed his own star and discovered the theory of relativity. Do not bury your ten talents; build on them. Use your time here to learn about nature, about God and His universe, and about His most beautiful creation, man. Look upon your fellow student as a friend, not an enemy. Truth is not petty and should not be hoarded, but shared. One of the greatest joys in knowing is to teach another. Let us learn to share according to the measure God has given us. Perhaps the great orator Cicero said it best: "Use what you have; that is the right way; do what is to be done in proportion as you have strength for it."

Member of the audience: To what extent does the university breed competition unknowingly—this university particularly and the higher education system in general—to the degree that competing with the Self in the way you suggest is very distant from most people coming into the educational environment? It seems to me that the type of competition that is called for on entering the academic environment is the destructive, negative kind as opposed to the kind you are speaking about.

Ms. Miller: Right. I think it is a learning procedure. I think it is part of the environment in which we grow up. I came here for my master's degree after being out of school for a number of years, and I could not believe the kind of competition that was going on in the undergraduate field. I had never seen anything like it before. It really was cutthroat. And you have to deal with that, and the only way you can deal with it is to say, "What am I going to get out of this myself? What do *I* want from this?" If I really want to learn, I have to deal with the dishonesty that is going on around me, and I have to accept it. Those people somehow will not know the material, or if they do know the material, they may not use it properly. There is always a balance.

Member of the audience: Recently, in doing women's studies, I was introduced to the idea that in the past men were very sensitive about being considered success objects in much the way women were opposed to being considered sex objects. With the whole movement of women's liberation and more women going into med school, graduate programs, etc., the whole notion of being success objects becomes more relevant to both men and women. Can you comment on this?

Ms. Miller: Well, I feel that I have competed and done what I have done in a very stressful environment, and I think that no matter what sex I was, I would have done the same thing because I found a reality about myself. I found a trueness about myself, and that success would be there no matter what body my soul happened to be in. I personally do not think that sex has anything to do with it. If that is the kind of competition that *you* have to deal with, then you have to find ways to feel comfortable with it—ways to feel good in your environment.

Father Robert Harvanek, S.J.: I found your attitude of competing with yourself a fruitful one. However, I wonder whether competition has not gotten a bad name in some circles without sufficient reflection. It is true that competition can lead to some undesirable results, and we see some of those at Loyola. However, competition is one of the natural stimuli to human achievement and personal progress. Competition is certainly essential to certain types of sport. In the realm of studies it was one of the features of the original Jesuit *Ratio Studiorum.* Would you say that competition with others is a useful and legitimate process in academe, or is it corruptive?

Ms. Miller: I truly do believe that competition is an essential part of the university, because we do have to find out where we are. We do have to find our standing in our environment, and that helps us to find what milieu, if you will, is most comfortable for us. Competition is essential to the human race, I'm afraid. It is something that maybe is instinctive—to try always to be better than someone else. I am not saying this does not exist or should not exist. I am saying that there may be a form of competition in some environments that could be better than the form we're using.

Father Donald Hayes, S.J.: Another question concerns a student's choice of goals. I think that, in the context of a liberal arts college, coming to grips with values or how a student makes decisions in the choice of this vocation over something else is an extremely important issue. A person who has all kinds of ability might be able to be a doctor or the president of a large corporation. It seems to me this is an important question that has to be looked at. How does one come to a decision? It has been mentioned that one could say, "I feel good with this decision." To some extent this may be true, but I would not want this to be interpreted to mean that emotions control my life—that I do something or make some decision only because "I feel good about it." Students and all of us, I hope, do not make decisions because "other people are doing it," "my parents want me to be a doctor," and so on. The Ignatian *Spiritual Exercises,* by the way, are precisely geared to train a person to make decisions for the right reasons.

Ms. Miller: And that is making a good person, is it not?

Father Hayes: Yes.

Dr. Ardis Collins: I would like to comment on the topic of competition for grades. To students I would say that in many departments of the university—certainly in the humanities core curriculum courses—the number of As available is not limited. Whoever earns an A can have one; you are competing against the professor's standards alone.

Ms. Miller: Perhaps I should have qualified my statement slightly. Certainly in graduate school it is not true that there are a limited number of As. When I was putting those words down on paper, I was thinking primarily of the very initial courses in college, which tend to weed out students who just can't deal with the academic situation.

Mr. McGinty: Thank you. Our next speaker will be Meg Kelly.

Honesty and Academia
Ms. Margaret Kelly, Mr. Mark Lauer
Mr. Michael O'Toole, Ms. Magdalen Belickas

Honesty, a trait that is integral to the Jesuit ideals, is in danger at Loyola University and other colleges across the country. An honesty that was historically cherished and even presupposed, especially in the academic world, has gradually declined in importance, to the detriment of academia. What, indeed, is this "honesty"? Why is it cherished by societies past and present? What has caused its decline, and what can we, as college students, do to reverse this process?

In our Western world, with its blending of the Greek and Christian traditions, truth as a value has always been an unavoidable virtue. The whole Greek system of ideas is based on the human desire to know. Everything else in life is meant to serve that purpose. Man is defined as a rational animal, and the ability to know is what differentiates this animal from other "lower" forms of life. The knowledge we are seeking is truth. In the Christian tradition, God is seen as the *logos*—the Word. He is all-knowing. "I am the Way, the Truth, and the Life." Christianity is based on communication. Man responds to God and expects a response from God. In this type of communication, honesty is presupposed.

The university as an institution was begun in a quest for truth and knowledge. It has its roots in the cathedral schools begun by the Emperor Charlemagne in the eighth and ninth centuries. As teaching and learning spread beyond the individual cathedral schools, the *studium generale* developed. Students from many parts of Europe would assemble in one specially renowned center of learning.

Higher education, where a select minority is instructed in special branches of knowledge, also took place in ancient Egypt, Greece, and Rome. Higher learning in Greece was based on the concept of the proper use of leisure time. The Greek word *schola* meant "leisure" or the activities of a freeman directed to the fullest appreciation of life. The term "liberal education," from the Latin *liber,* meaning "free," parallels this Greek notion as contrasted with "vocational" or "professional" education, which prepares us to earn a living. In the Greek scholastic system, the question of honesty was a question of personal integrity. Since those early beginnings, the university as a center for study has blossomed; yet much personalization has been lost. We are now faced with a mass-produced education in which honesty is not only a question for each individual, but a question that affects the entire academic community.

As we begin a new decade, it is important that we take stock of our past and present and the direction of our future. It is our finding that the past and present have a problem that only our future will help to decide. The problem has plagued man from the beginning in all phases of interpersonal relations. The problem of honesty in a particular setting, Loyola University, is our concern.

Within our society today, there is a traceable trend to the relaxation of honesty as a value. This value has long been believed in and taught by both the academic community and members of the Society of Jesus. The very essence of honesty is being challenged at the individual level. The individual has begun to question and challenge, and, in the end, to rationalize the decline of honesty as a highly held value.

In the application of this notion to Loyola University, it is important to ask what is happening to our ethics and values. Are we shut off from the influence of the outside world so that a general societal decline in values has no effect on us? If not, then where are these effects being felt, and how are we dealing with them? These are questions that in one sense are only the top layer, yet at the same time are the base of the matter.

The decline in values and ethics in the society has a parallel in this academic community. We feel justified in saying that this decline has affected all phases of the university—students, faculty, and administration. But honesty appears to have been abandoned most markedly within the student population. Reports of plagiarism, stealing, cheating, and the much-publicized West Point incident fill the pages of newspapers and the desks of deans. It appears that honesty no longer holds a place of importance. However, another decline can be closely related to that of honesty—that of the quest for an education in its most pure sense.

It is not our intention to outline the individual problems that plague Loyola University; rather it is our goal to present general trends that we see and to construct solutions for them.

In the present academic world, there is an increased movement towards the postgraduate and professional institutions. This movement causes the undergraduate educators to gear their curriculum towards these receiving institutions, which forces them to see themselves in a different role. The economic market of today demands that educational institutions establish criteria by which the marketplace can decide who will be the better worker among its future executives and professionals. The academic institution finds itself in a Catch-22 situation, for if it is to remain viable, it must respond to the demands of the financial sector of society. Yet these demands cause the university to differentiate among students for someone else's sake. Now we must ask what are the prices that the university and the students have to pay for having to succumb to some of the pressures of the economic marketplace and the receiving institutions.

Undergraduates no longer have the option of taking courses that merely interest them; they are being forced to take more required courses that will prepare them for possible positions in a graduate program. With this narrow outlook, the elements of a Jesuit liberal arts education become secondary goals for many students and faculty members.

As stated in the undergraduate catalog of Loyola University:

The Jesuit tradition, as embodied at Loyola, emphasizes the development of the individual student, including social, moral, and spiritual growth within the Judaeo-Christian framework. The goal of Jesuit higher education is men and women who are intellectually mature, whose lives express the values which they embrace, who spend themselves in service to their fellow man, and who view their good works as a contribution to the glory of God. As a Catholic university, Loyola's objective is to be a Christian presence in institutional form in the academic world and to confront the major problems of our day. Every academic program at Loyola stresses a broad liberal arts background, which is considered to be the base from which all students can branch out into special interests, specific fields, and vocations.

In a liberal arts education, we feel the single most important tool that helps students to reinforce their values, most importantly honesty, is the core curriculum. The core can and should develop and challenge those values learned or handed down from family, peers, and religious affiliations. It should add an intellectual and deeper understanding of what values such as honesty are in the eventual hope of making those values truly one's own—not just borrowed. However, there is an obvious tension between the idea of what the core curriculum should achieve and what it does achieve. The core is looked upon by many students as something to "get out of the way" so the "real" learning can go on. However, the core is one of the most valuable tools that the Loyola community has in its training of the young men and women who are to meet the challenges of the coming decade. A misunderstanding of the core's intended purpose by both faculty and students has created a crisis in the furthering of liberal arts education and has led to an atmosphere where values such as honesty have declined. Loyola University is in danger of allowing the values learned from a liberal arts education to slip into second place behind postgraduate competition in the academic sphere. This crisis is not without a solution. But it is a solution that involves costs; it demands resources, human input, and human creativity on the part of the entire university community.

The university must decide as a whole that it will accept this challenge. It must be a total university effort with the cooperation of everyone. Loyola must immediately begin to stress the value and importance of a liberal arts education.

The admissions information must emphasize that Loyola is, first and foremost, educating its students so as to afford them the opportunity to lead a full and good human life. Secondly, Loyola is concerned with educating students in their specialties. Loyola must begin to recruit and attract the kind of student who is open-minded to all disciplines and willing to explore new ideas. Loyola may have to give less promotion to success in medical and dental school acceptances. This is an important aspect of our academic community, but it should not be the most important point. We must realize that we are educating people for life—not to become doctors and dentists. Other institutions are accredited to do that.

To achieve this goal of a better realization of the purposes and intent of the core, we suggest a reeducation about the value of the core for both faculty and students. One suggestion would be a short course required of all students in their first year that would explain the purpose and philosophy of a liberal arts education. As mentioned earlier, we believe many of the difficulties, such as dishonesty, in our educational system arise from a perceived conflict between preprofessionalism and a complete liberal arts education. What better way to remedy this conflict than through a one-hour course designed for that purpose? A freshman counseling system is not enough; there must be some concrete, thought-provoking follow-up.

If Loyola were to adopt this idea and stress these values throughout its entire educational system, we feel an attitudinal change would occur within the student body. The students who are enrolling will realize that they are embarking on an adventure, that the challenge presented to them will be great, and that much will be expected of them. We feel the students will rise to meet this challenge.

Loyola University will eventually produce a student who is able to embody the values and ethics of a Jesuit liberal arts education. The university will produce alumni who believe in and are able to make a difference in the rediscovery of the morals and values of our society. The dishonesty that is an unfortunate by-product of the pressures generated by a misunderstanding of a liberal arts education should begin to diminish. We feel there would be less of a cutthroat attitude among students because many would realize the importance of the total educational experience. As long as man is human and vulnerable to pressures, both internally and externally, there will always be dishonesty. But much of this problem can be alleviated by reducing those pressures that our institutional system appears to be fostering.

Yet how do we face the immediate crisis of academic dishonesty within our academic community? Since our proposal may take many years to accomplish and involves in many ways an attitudinal change that will inevitably be slow, we are now faced with the problem of what we can do at the present time to upgrade the value and quality of our educational system.

Loyola University has recognized the problem of academic honesty within its community. In 1978 it responded by establishing a committee composed of faculty and students. The committee recommended that a new statement concerning academic honesty be placed in the undergraduate catalog. This statement reads, and I quote,

> Academic honesty demands that the pursuit of knowledge in the university be carried on with sincerity and honesty. At the core of the university lies an implied contract between student and teacher. The teacher agrees to guide the student in acquiring knowledge, skills, and competencies. The student agrees to do those activities which the teacher considers appropriate for learning in an ethical way. When either teacher or student fails to abide by the implied contract, academic honesty is in jeopardy.

As defined in this statement, academic honesty is indeed in jeopardy at Loyola University. The contract between teacher and student is broken on one side or the other nearly every day. Who should be responsible for enforcing this contract? Should it be up to the university to impose a moral sanction regarding honesty? Should it be left to the discretion of the individual student or faculty member?

The basic agreement between faculty member and student may be broken in many ways. Students may cheat directly: copying test answers, copying homework, stealing exams, or plagiarizing papers. Others may cheat more indirectly: refusing to share notes, not helping a fellow student, or "brownnosing" teachers. As our grammar school teachers told us time and time again, these people are only cheating themselves. This is sad but true.

Students who do this year after year are depriving themselves of the challenge of a good education. They are not expanding their knowledge; they are simply "getting by." They are not exercising themselves to their full potential, and they are indeed wasting what may very well be one of their last opportunities to be exposed to so many different disciplines. And yet most of these students feel completely content with what they are doing. They are going to get into professional school.

When faculty members are inadequately prepared for a class or do not update course materials, they fail to live up to their agreement with their students. By not always providing students with an accurate course syllabus, professors provide the opportunity for students to perceive the course incorrectly. Professors should make themselves available to students in scheduled office hours so that academic matters can be discussed. Examinations given in each course should accurately test a student's knowledge of the assigned material. These examinations should be changed from year to year so as to afford each student an equal opportunity to do well.

We propose an across-the-board stated policy on cheating, especially concerning tests and plagiarism. It is important that the university put forth a detailed set of procedures of what a faculty member or student is to do in the cases when academic dishonesty is suspected. The procedural investigation should include both faculty and students and should be standard—not up to the individual or department.

Although faculty members should not be expected to be policemen or baby-sitters, we feel that they have a very definite obligation to take every reasonable step to ensure that the class is as free as possible from dishonesty. Not only do we believe that faculty members should be encouraged to ensure honesty, but guidelines should also be set up that require an educational atmosphere where honesty prevails. Recommendations for these guidelines could include: a strict limit to class size, a fixed proctor-student ratio for all tests, an avoidance of computerized testing when possible, multiple versions of the same tests, and special seating arrangements. Although these suggestions would require more work for all involved, they would be conducive to an honest academic atmosphere for all but the most ardent cheaters. Such an atmosphere is necessary if academia is to maintain its high standards, and until such an atmosphere can be achieved through attitudinal changes, it must be enforced with strict guidelines and severe penalties.

Mr. McGinty: Thank you, Meg. Meg's coauthors will also be answering questions. We'd like to open up the discussion at this time.

Dr. David Tribble: Something bothers me about what is being said here today. It seems to me that you are going to treat the symptoms and not the causes. The reason I say this is that the first speaker painted a picture for us of what a liberal education should be: the goals, values, etc. And she intimated that when a student comes from high school to college, the student does not understand the values of the system. You yourself, Ms. Kelly, have said that there is a "perceived conflict" between preprofessional education and liberal education. Now it seems to me *there* is the cause of dishonesty. If we want to get at the cause, why not look at that conflict? If there is a real conflict, then throw the preprofessional students out. If, however, this is a perceived conflict and not real, we are allowing students to come into our institutions with the wrong ideas and doing nothing about it. I'd like your comment.

Mr. Mark Lauer: I believe that in our presentation we did make this point. To help alleviate the problem, we would suggest that within the first semester at Loyola, a student, whether a freshman, sophomore, junior, or senior, have a one-hour course on exactly what a liberal arts education is—how it is to be perceived in itself and as related to preprofessionalism. People should come to know exactly what they're getting into and what Loyola is trying to accomplish. And we feel that this should be done in the first semester a student spends here.

Dr. Tribble: Would you say that the conflict is real?

Mr. Lauer: I would say it's real.

Dr. Tribble: You are saying that there is a real, fundamental conflict between preprofessional education and liberal education?

Mr. Lauer: Right now within the student body—yes. Yes, many students just want to get the core out of the way.

Dr. Tribble: Now you're talking about how they perceive it. They perceive it as a conflict? Do you believe there is an inherent conflict?

Mr. Lauer: I don't believe that there is an *inherent* conflict. But if we're going to handle the problem specific to Loyola, the problem is that there is a perceived conflict, and we have to deal with it.

Mr. Michael O'Toole: Can I make one more comment on that? I don't think that there is a conflict between what a professional school should want and what a liberal arts education should produce. The problem arises when you have students coming into an educational system such as Loyola University who really do not understand what a liberal arts education is trying to achieve. They hear things from peers, family, people who have gone through this before, and there is a lot of misinformation. What we suggested was to try to get them in freshman year when they're really forming their perception of what college life is and of what a medical school, dental school, or law school, etc., will be looking for. Quite fortunately, this is a *perceived* conflict. The conflict should not be there. The eventual result of a liberal arts education should agree with the objectives of a professional school or a good Christian life.

Dr. Robert Black: I am Dr. Black from the dental school. We want the person with a liberal arts education. The fact that there are certain courses that students have to have before they get into dental school does not mean that we only want science students. We want a liberal education, and I think we have it in our student body. I think it is important to have a religious emphasis on professional things. I sometimes think that dentistry probably demands more morality and more ethics than almost any other profession. What I do is between you and me, and you don't know what I'm doing. The physician's work is observed by nurses trained in medicine and by other physicians; lawyers are observed by other lawyers or by judges. But really there is no one looking over *our* shoulders. Therefore, I think, we need more morality, more ethics in my profession—I'm probably prejudiced—but I think we do. I'd hate to see our education and our dental school given over to a nonreligious institution such as a state school.

Dr. Suzanne Gossett: I have another question. You're proposing a one-hour addition to the core. But it seems to me that we are dealing with an extremely serious structural problem that none of you has quite addressed. Someone made a comment about mass-produced education. If I'm correct, what we have is *not* mass-produced education. We have education for the masses. What has happened historically in America is that a larger and larger percentage of people of college age are going on to college. At a certain time when I was in England, 6 percent of people between ages eighteen and twenty-two were in some institution of higher learning, whereas at that time, which is many years ago, 35 percent of Americans between ages eighteen and twenty-two were in institutions of higher learning. Now what we've seen in the past fifteen years is an increase of pressure on the undergraduate institution, with more and more people coming in, while there has been a more or less contained number of graduate students, especially professional students. I know that we need a critical number of students to run a university like Loyola, yet maybe what we need is more competition to get in here first. Then we wouldn't have so many problems with the students who are here. I've heard a great deal about plagiarism by people trying to get into medical school—that seems to be the stereotype. What I've discovered in my classes, however, is that straightforward plagiarism is most frequently done by people who cannot hack it, just cannot make the minimum standards. Do you really think a one-hour course is going to reply to this kind of massive structural problem?

Mr. O'Toole: We are not looking for *the* solution. The point we are trying to hit was the misperception of what a liberal arts education is and the preprofessionalism that pervades the entire university. And we're looking at ways to deal with this problem. We're not saying that we have *the* solution. A one-hour course, I think, would help to clear up this conflict between liberal arts and preprofessionalism. We also touched upon other points that could help solve this. The admissions policy of Loyola really emphasizes the preprofessional nature of the school, and I can see the necessity of this to bring in students. A university needs a certain number of students to function and to be able to provide services. But there has to be some balancing. The emphasis on a liberal arts education really has to be there.

Mr. McGinty: Our final paper is presented by Kevin Coley.

Persons-for-Others
Mr. Kevin Coley, Mr. Terry Johnson

In his book *The Body—a Study in Pauline Theology,* J. A. T. Robinson maintains that if we, the human race, are to survive at all it can only be as "members one of another."

Robinson's message is fundamentally a call to interdependence. It calls us to acknowledge and respect the fact that the human race is one body, an interconnected whole. It calls us to become increasingly aware of the extent to which the actions of one member of the body affect the other members. Finally, it is an urgent call to live in greater harmony with the body as a whole.

We believe Robinson's words pose a critical challenge to the future of our country in general and, more particularly, to the future of Jesuit higher education as it is expressed here at Loyola University of Chicago.

To begin with, let us examine how this call challenges the American ideal of individualism. This ideal, sometimes viewed as isolationist, has been a constant thread throughout our American political tradition. Our willingness to aid others has always been tempered by our desire to protect our primarily national interests above all other concerns. When faced with an issue of global import, we have tended to weigh possible solutions solely on the basis of their national ramifications rather than their wider world impact. This phenomenon has surfaced once again with regard to the current oil crisis, as exemplified by a recent oil company advertisement stating that "America runs better on American oil."

Because of the political and social constraints currently felt by both our nation and the world community, individualism no longer remains a viable policy option. The pressure of an ever-increasing population relying on steadily decreasing supplies of food and natural resources has destroyed the myth that one nation can survive apart from the rest of the world. A dynamic tension exists among all nations, rendering each of them a member of a larger whole.

What response, then, is predicated by this new awareness? We as a nation must accept, and work to strengthen, our interdependent relationship with the other nations of the world. As individuals we must become increasingly responsible members of our small immediate communities, of our present academic community, and of our global community.

It is here that the role of institutions of higher education becomes all-important. The task of educating the students of today to this new reality falls to the university. This challenge speaks most directly to Jesuit institutions, for their tradition is deeply rooted in an attitude of service to others.

What exactly is this Ignatian vision of which we speak? As traditionally defined, it can be seen as an invitation to exist in service to others. The individual is called to the development of the world into the Kingdom of God.

The essence of Ignatius' vision is linked to a belief in God's plan for our world. We are, according to Ignatius, involved in a divine drama. We are invited to participate actively in this drama, contributing to the gradual reshaping of the world to its divine design.

The purpose of the Jesuit university, then, has traditionally been to introduce young people to this world view and to encourage them to find their place in the unfolding process, to become participants in the divine design. In the light of our current emphasis on interdependence, it may be noted here that concern for the well-being of others has always been central to this transforming process.

This task of communicating a spiritually oriented world view was much less complex in the past than it is now. As recently as twenty years ago, the vast majority of the faculty were Jesuits who shared a common language and tradition. Further, the tight curriculum gave an integrated view of human life and divine purpose, seeing the former as an expression of the latter.

We are in a very different position today. Jesuits represent but a small percentage of the faculty, and the curriculum has been strained in an attempt to incorporate the ever-growing demands of academic specialties, preprofessional competence, and non-Jesuit influences. As a result, the university is marked by diversity and pluralism in terms of language, traditions, beliefs, and orientation.

In the face of this new pressure of diversity, the following questions arise: Has the vision of Ignatius remained central to the Loyola educational process? Does Loyola today serve as an articulator of the Ignatian call to interdependence? The answers to these questions may be examined on each of two levels: What is the philosophical commitment made by Loyola today, and to what extent is this commitment carried out in practice?

On the philosophical level, commitment to concern for others is very much a part of the established standards of the university. The ideal towards which the institution strives, as set forth in the 1979–1981 undergraduate catalog, is of the very essence of Ignatian thought.

> Our prime educational objectives are to form: "persons-for-others"; persons who are fashioned in the new humanism, the first principle of which is responsibility to our brothers and to history, cognizant of the present situation of human society, and actively concerned for the future of the human race; . . . persons formed in love with a passion for justice; persons capable of enjoying life in its highest forms.

Such words, however noble, remain but empty platitudes unless an attempt is made to integrate this philosophy concretely into the university's day-to-day operations. Words speak to the intellect. The university must present an invitation to its members aimed at their emotional beings, in the hope of sparking a deeper personal commitment to the ideals expressed in that invitation. Later we will discuss the possible responses of the individual. Let us now consider, however, the extent to which this invitation is being presented.

There are, as we see it, three aspects to Loyola's attempt to bring the Ignatian vision alive for its members: its commitment to the core curriculum and the ideals it embodies, the establishment of forums for debates, and the support of many and varied action-oriented programs.

Foremost among these is the commitment to the core curriculum. At a time when numerous other institutions of higher education are lessening or abandoning their core requirements, Loyola has chosen to maintain and strengthen hers. It is this core that serves as the basic foundation of the Jesuit education Loyola professes to offer. It seeks to educate individuals versed in all areas of learning, able to integrate the varied, seemingly unrelated array of material presented them into a coherent whole. An individual thus trained is able to grasp the complexities of the interdependent world situation and to become more capable of operating within its framework. Thus, while seeming to many to be but a mindless drudgery, the core serves to produce individuals better qualified to deal with the issues of the so-called "outside world."

Forums for debate, such as the Academic Council and the University Committee on Hunger, allow for the enlightened exchange of ideas that brings about a deeper understanding of the question at hand for all concerned. This symposium is a prime example. Its purpose is not to outline plans of action but to initiate discussion of those issues that pose a crucial threat to the idea of education as it is expressed here at Loyola. In the words of a well-known philosopher: "It is better to debate a question without settling it than to settle it without debate."

Action programs are perhaps the most visible aspect of Loyola's commitment to the Ignatian vision of interdependence. Events such as Hunger Week and the Rape Awareness Program afford the individual the opportunity to become actively involved in the problems confronting the community and the world surrounding Loyola. The participating individual is forced to become aware of the realities of our world situation and, at the same time, to become aware of the effectiveness of individual and communal action.

Such programs are by their very nature, however, short-lived: the commitment required of the individual, however intense, is brief. Loyola does present avenues calling for a more lasting commitment on the part of the individual. On the faculty level there is the Walk-to-Work program, which calls for a somewhat permanent commitment to the betterment of the surrounding community. On the student level this can best be seen in the university's support of University Ministry, many of whose programs call for an ongoing commitment. Examples of such programs are the newly formed Social Justice Task Force and the community living environment fostered on the community floors of Mertz Hall and in Gonzaga Hall.

As suggested previously, these efforts are but invitations to action; it remains the prerogative of the individual to accept the responsibility of his or her interdependence with the members of both immediate and world communities. What avenues exist through which the individual can act to accept this responsibility and bring the resulting commitment alive for others?

On the faculty level we have identified three such avenues. First, there is a constant challenge for faculty members to expand their areas of research, for it is through research that new ideas and means to combat social suffering are unearthed. Secondly, they should constantly strive to provide an effective forum for debate within their classrooms. Students are not merely receptacles of knowledge; they should be challenged to come to their own understanding of the material being presented. In this way both parties come to a deeper understanding of the material, and the student develops the ability to present and defend his or her thoughts. Finally, faculty members should strive to make connections between the material they present and the larger body of knowledge, wisdom, and values embraced by the university. No idea is developed in a vacuum. The student should be made aware of the effect of an author's understanding of the world, the evolution of the theory throughout history, and its effects on those who were in some way influenced by it. In this way the student will be able to judge the material by its contribution to the evolution of thought.

For the student there exist two somewhat interrelated levels of commitment, apart from the obvious commitment to academic development. First, there is service in action-oriented programs, whose benefits have already been enumerated. Such a commitment, however, is but the tip of the iceberg. As stated previously, such programs generally call for a short-term commitment. Even so, some students are prevented from participating in these programs due to pressures of school, work, and family. Does this mean they are excluded from any attempt to bring the Ignatian vision alive?

No! Just as there is no "typical" Jesuit, there is no "typical" Jesuit student. Ignatius saw many varied ways of bringing his vision alive, and this fact must be respected. What is required, however, is that this commitment be expanded through all levels of the individual's life. A real attempt must be made to incorporate the skills of being a person-for-others into one's everyday experiences. The call to interdependence is more than a temporary commitment to a specific action program. It calls for a constant commitment to the ideals of interdependence, a constant concern for the well-being of others.

We have mentioned only a few of the areas in which the university and its members may work to actualize the ideals and values they express. We believe it is imperative that the university continue to develop creative means of integrating the interdependent vision of Ignatius into its everyday actions, and that the individuals within the university should actively strive to incorporate this vision into their everyday lives. We value the struggle to maintain the standards upon which Loyola prides herself and encourage a further deepening of the commitment these standards represent. We further recognize and value Loyola's struggle to maintain a creative tension between offering a substantive and marketable education and a broad, tested vision of life.

We propose no single course of action; rather, we hope to encourage the further development of the rich diversity that marks the Loyola University of 1980. Our purpose this afternoon has been to stimulate discussion both within and among the individual members of the Loyola community. All should question Loyola's commitment to the Ignatian vision so as to ensure its continued vitality. Faculty members should ask themselves whether they enter their classrooms merely to impart knowledge or truly to educate their students. Students should question their reasons for seeking an education. Do they desire knowledge so that they can reap its benefits, or do they desire to gain more to give to others? It is our hope that this, and all the other presentations of this symposium, will serve to reaffirm Loyola's commitment to the Ignatian vision of interdependence and to strengthen our individual resolve to commit ourselves to becoming persons-for-others.

Mr. McGinty: We open up the floor for questions.

Member of the audience: Your emphasis on interdependence invites some inspection of the things that were said earlier. One is that cheaters cheat themselves, and that that's their worst punishment. They cheat you, too. They destroy and erode the quality of the education that you get, and they keep you from getting the quality of competition that you should have for your own best development. Until you see that they're cheating you as well as themselves, interdependence is not expressed. Likewise, in that true competition that is your competition against yourself, unless you can identify yourself as interdependent with the larger community, you have settled for a smaller self than the self with which you should come out of here.

Mr. Terry Johnson: That's a point well taken.

Editor: There followed audience discussion on various purposes for research—for example, to improve instruction, to acquire new knowledge, and to improve the quality of life. Because the tapes simply do not allow for an accurate transcription, I have omitted that discussion.

PANEL 4
Seated: Ms. Marilyn Birchfield
and Dr. David Ozar

Standing:
Dr. William Donnelly,
Dr. Thomas Donaldson,
Mr. Charles Murdock,
Dr. Alan Fredian,
Mr. Joseph Lassner
(from left to right)

PANEL 4

Teaching Ethics in the University:
A Reflection of Aims
Dr. David Ozar

Moderator:
Mr. Charles Murdock
Panelists:
Ms. Marilyn Birchfield
Dr. Thomas Donaldson
Dr. William J. Donnelly
Dr. Alan J. Fredian
Mr. Joseph Lassner

Mr. Charles Murdock: I am Bud Murdock, dean of the Law
School, and it is my pleasure this afternoon to moderate
the fourth panel in this series. While it is always risky to
attempt to summarize what has gone before, in a sense
the first week was a more theoretical approach to the
subject, whereas today we are attempting to concretize some
of the ideas developed last week. The previous session was
from the students' perspective, and this session will be from
the perspective of faculty members concerned in one way or
another with the teaching of ethics within the university.
Leading off our program is Professor David Ozar, of the
Department of Philosophy, who will present his paper; then
each of the panelists will respond. That will leave one half
hour for questions, and the burden of going forward will then
fall upon you, the audience.

Dr. David Ozar is an associate professor of philosophy at Loyola. He has undergraduate and graduate degrees from Loyola, and his Ph.D. is from Yale University. Before joining us, he taught at Marygrove College in Detroit. His published work is in the area of ethics, social philosophy, and the philosophy of law. He has also been active in writing and speaking on the teaching of ethics. He will speak to us now on "Teaching Ethics in the University: A Reflection of Aims." Dr. David Ozar.

Teaching Ethics in the University: A Reflection of Aims
Dr. David Ozar

There are many of us in the university who are engaged in one way or another in teaching ethics. I am not just talking about classes formally titled "Ethics" in the philosophy department or "Moral Theology" in the theology department, for many Loyola faculty members in many divisions of the university are concerned to increase their students' awareness of the moral issues involved in or related to their particular subject matter; and the university as a whole has a long-standing commitment that its formative influence develop not only the students' intellectual and social capacities, but their moral capacities as well.

Given the extent of our efforts to teach ethics in this university, and given the depth of the university's commitment to this enterprise, it is important to have a clear sense of what our aims are. The task which I have set for myself today is to describe the aims that we may properly and realistically pursue in our teaching of ethics in the university. My guiding example will be drawn from the field of medical ethics, and the commentators who will speak after me will focus on several of Loyola's professional programs. We hope that what we shall say will illuminate the proper and realistic aims of all the different activities by which ethics is taught in the university.

I want to begin with a story, a story about myself. This past fall, shortly after Labor Day, my father, who is seventy-five, suffered a series of strokes, including finally a very severe one. He was in critical condition for five days. I was with him during that time and, since I am the only child and my mother is deceased, I was the one responsible for making decisions regarding his care.

On the day when my father's condition turned critical, when the stroke brought on a frightening round of grand mal seizures that medication could not control, my father's doctor asked me how I wanted the hospital staff to respond in the event that my father's heart or respiration should stop. Should the staff begin cardiopulmonary resuscitation and call for the emergency cart and the respirator, or should they let things be?

Now I had been teaching courses in medical ethics at that point for five years. I had studied, reflected on, and discussed these issues a great deal. Yet when the doctor asked me that question, it floored me.

It was not that the question surprised me in any way. With a little foresight, I could easily have seen it coming. In fact my first reaction to the question was to say to myself, "Of course! This question has to be answered." And it was also clear to me that I was the one who had to answer it, so I was not surprised that I was the one being asked the question.

No; what floored me was the question itself. Was my father to be resuscitated if his heart or breathing stopped, or not? When this question was addressed to me, about my father, I did not know how to answer it. I remember saying to a friend that evening, while I was still trying to determine how I would respond, "I've been teaching medical ethics for five years. But when it's your own family, when the question is actually asked of you about your own father, all that academic experience isn't worth much."

During the next two days, through a great deal of reflection and conversation, and prayer and anguish, with the help of my wife and several good friends and a couple of the nurses on the floor, I worked the matter out for myself, and I made a choice, a choice with which I am sure my father would have agreed. I chose that heroic lifesaving measures not be undertaken, that cardiopulmonary resuscitation not be administered if my father's heart or breathing should stop, that the emergency cart and the respirator not be called.

As it happened, my father's seizures stopped. After several days his condition stabilized, and he came off the critical list.

Five weeks later he moved to a nursing home, and in mid-January he moved into a retirement home. Physically he has recovered from the stroke almost completely, though he still suffers from a partial language disability called aphasia that was caused by the stroke. All in all, his recovery has been remarkable.

So my order not to resuscitate, which I had agonized over so much, never had to be used. But I need not tell you that I have not forgotten the experience of facing that question, for many reasons.

One particular reason that is relevant to our enterprise here today concerns my comment to my friend that all my academic experience with issues in medical ethics seemed not to be worth much when that question was actually asked of me about my own father. For if I have not profited from all that experience, surely my students have not profited from it either. Yet I am sure that I have done some good by my teaching; and the students seem to think so too, not only during each course, but when I hear from them afterwards as well.

So I have come to ask myself once again, in a fresh way, what it is that teachers of ethics can do for their students—and for themselves—when they teach? What is the relation of the teaching of ethics in a university to actual decision-making situations in which the students—and their teachers—will find themselves as they live their lives? If I have benefited from my experience with the issues of medical ethics, then why was I so much at a loss when the question whether or not to resuscitate was actually asked of me? In sum, what should be the aims of those who teach ethics in the university? What aims are proper, and what aims are realistically attainable?

At first look it might seem very natural to say that the proper aim of those who teach ethics is to provide their students with answers to important moral or ethical questions and in this way to show their students how they are to act in various morally complex situations. But further reflection shows, I think, that, though this is a natural enough answer, still it is not the proper aim of the teaching of ethics, and it is not a realistic aim either. It is not the proper aim because a morally mature person is not one whose head is packed with specific responses for specific situations. Rather, the morally mature person is one who is sensitive to the moral components of the situations that arise, who recognizes the values and moral principles that are at stake in these situations, and who can judge the merits and demerits of the various courses of action that are available in terms of these values and moral principles. The morally mature person is one who can reason clearly about these matters, who can form sound judgments about them, and who can make responsible choices. None of this suggests that the morally mature person knows in advance how he or she will respond to each particular situation that might arise. This is why we contribute precious little to the growth of moral maturity if our teaching of ethics is nothing more than directions to our students on how to act in this type of situation or that. Nor is it surprising that our students resent teaching of this sort about moral or ethical matters and that they resist it, because such an approach focuses so little on the students' development of their own moral powers.

This idea—that teachers of ethics should aim at telling students how to respond to various kinds of particular situations—is unrealistic as well. In the first place, there is no way that we who teach can foresee the specific kinds of situations our students will face. We can offer sample cases for discussion, but we would be naive to think that our students—or we ourselves—will actually face the exact situations we propose for study. In addition, when I face a real choice situation, the final judgment about the situation will have to be my judgment and the final choice will be my choice. For in real choice situations, the resolution of the situation depends on me. No amount of classroom discussion of cases or of giving our students directions on how to act in particular situations can possibly imitate this feature of the real choice situation. And that is why, again, the emphasis in our teaching of ethics must be on the formation of our students' powers of sound judgment and responsible choice rather than on trying to give them final answers to questions about particular kinds of situations.

In addition, though it may seem strange for me to say this, I do not find it at all difficult to imagine that another person who was in exactly the same position with regard to his or her father that I was in with regard to mine, and who approached that situation just as carefully and conscientiously as I tried to do, might well have reached a different final judgment and made a different choice from my own. I can conceive of that person's judgment and choice having been just as sound and responsible as my own, even though different. For it seems to me that there are situations—and the type of situation that I was in with regard to my father could easily have been one of them—in which morally mature and conscientious people, even though they respond to the same basic values and the same fundamental moral principles, may nevertheless disagree about the proper resolution of a particular morally complex feature of a situation and may in fact disagree without either of them being able to say that the other is clearly wrong.

I am certainly not saying that every answer about every morally complex situation is just as good as every other answer. But I am saying that there are situations in which even the most careful and conscientious examination of the values and moral principles involved may nevertheless fail to yield a single resolution of the situation that is clearly the best but may yield instead a set of several alternative resolutions, resolutions that are clearly better than any other possibilities, but are mutually exclusive and cannot be successfully ranked one above the other. In such situations morally mature and conscientious men and women may well choose differently, either choosing different courses of action from among those that are equally good, equally valued, equally obligatory, or choosing to prefer one value or principle over another that is of equal significance and adopting the course of action that is in accord with that choice.

The fact that this is so leads me as a teacher of ethics to be extremely hesitant to offer my own judgment of a particular moral issue to my students as a rule to guide their actions. For I can conceive that other persons, just as morally mature and conscientious as I try to be, might come to a different judgment about this particular case, one which my students ought to be aware of. Far better, it seems to me, that the teacher of ethics present his or her judgments about moral questions as examples of a process, trying to be aware of the values and moral principles that are involved, and of a process growing in one's moral powers of clear reasoning, sound judgment, and responsible choice—that is, as examples of processes in which the teacher, as a fallible but somewhat educated and somewhat sensitive human being, is engaged in and trying to carry out well. Far better this, I believe, than offering one's own or anyone else's judgments of moral issues as the last word and as a rule to tell one's students how they are to act.

I have spent considerable time criticizing what I think is a natural, but mistaken, view of the aim of teaching ethics. Let me now address the question about aims more constructively. I wish to describe four aims that I think can actually be achieved in practice, which are, in my view, the proper aims of those who teach ethics in the university.

The first of these aims concerns something that I have already spoken of: a person's awareness of and sensitivity to the values and moral principles that are at stake in the concrete situations of his or her life. It is all too easy for us to look on and estimate the choice situations of our lives from the point of view of a very narrow range of concerns. We commonly think of children as being morally immature because the range of values and principles of conduct that they are aware of is so limited. But even widely experienced adults often have no broader a scope than children in the values and principles of conduct that they attend to seriously, though the adult's narrowness is often quite different from the child's.

One particular kind of adult narrowness that deserves special mention is the tendency of many adults to judge their own and others' actions almost exclusively in terms of *performance.* By this I mean a tendency to judge actions in terms of successful performance of the tasks that are associated with a particular role or type of work where success is measured by criteria internal to the role or the task itself, and not in terms of other values and moral principles that might be relevant. The businessman who is judged and judges others primarily in terms of profit margin or volume of sales; the lawyer who is judged and judges others primarily in terms of number and public prominence of clients or cases won; the professor who is judged and judges others primarily in terms of scholarly papers read and articles published; the student who is judged and judges others primarily in terms of grade point average and number of medical school interviews—these are examples—and we could easily name many others—of people who overlook a wide range of values and moral principles that are relevant to what they do.

Some of our students in the university, like some proportion of adults everywhere, are still narrow in childish ways. But most of our students, like most of us who teach them, are narrow more by having taken the bait of performance as the spontaneous criterion of our own and others' conduct. So we all need to have our awareness of and sensitivity to the values and moral principles that are involved in what we do heightened and strengthened.

Thus the natural scientist, for example, rightly works to enhance his or her students' awe at the wonders of nature and to form them in the methods that will enable them to expand our understanding of those wonders. But the natural scientist can also work to raise in the students' minds the question whether what is learned in this or that program of research has any chance of benefiting human beings and whether the effort, time, and physical resources are worth the result. Such a question may be answerable by educated guesses at best, but that is no reason for not asking it. The question is of constant importance, for it reminds teacher and students alike that there are other values besides the advancement of science and that those studying the sciences must work to keep themselves aware that this is so.

The same can be said, to take a second example, of those who teach in the social and behavioral sciences, but here there is an added dimension of awareness of values that comes immediately to mind. For the subjects of research in the social and behavioral sciences are frequently human beings. So, besides raising for discussion with their students the question whether particular programs of research will significantly benefit anyone and whether they are therefore worth the effort, time, and resources expended on them, teachers in the social and behavioral sciences ought to direct their students' attention to questions regarding informed consent on the part of research subjects and to issues regarding other fundamental rights of subjects that various research techniques and activities might violate.

We could easily multiply such examples by looking to other fields of teaching and research, but let me simply make my point. Teaching the students what has been learned in a field up to now and teaching them how to gather and interpret new information is so massive a task and requires such effort and concentration that we who teach can easily overlook the value considerations and moral issues involved in or related to our subject matter. But our teaching is surely incomplete if it does not increase our students' awareness that value considerations and moral issues are involved. For all growth of our students' moral powers depends on increasing this basic awareness.

Remember that I am not talking about giving final answers to moral questions; I have made that point very strongly. I am talking about helping our students and ourselves become more aware of the moral questions that are there, waiting to be addressed. All that we have to do is to call attention to the values or moral principles that are at stake. Doing that is really rather easy. It is getting ourselves to do it that is hard, because that requires changing our patterns, interrupting the usual way we do things, teaching one thing less so that the moral dimensions of another can be attended to. It requires us to work actively against the tendency to say, "I have too much to do already," by frankly doing less of something to do more of this.

I have to say that this works. It is my experience that if we are modest, if we do not claim that we have all the answers, and if we act from a sincere concern about the values and moral principles to which we call our students' attention, we will find them responsive, concerned about the issues that are raised, interested in the values and moral principles that are at stake, and even grateful for the chance to give these matters some thought. Thus, the first aim of teaching ethics in the university is the easiest of the four to achieve, and it is also the most important, since the rest all depend on it.

The second aim I shall speak of concerns the strengthening of our students' powers of clear and careful reasoning with regard to moral matters. Clear and careful reasoning is sometimes a matter of some subtlety, and there may be some who believe that teaching students to reason clearly and carefully is a task to be left chiefly to philosophers or mathematicians. But every academic discipline has its theoretical component, and we have all had to demonstrate our capacity to think and write in a logical manner. And at root it is simply the capacity to think logically about moral matters that we are talking about. When we raise these issues with our students, we can help them grow in the power of clear and careful reasoning by listening carefully to ourselves and to them, by making sure that what we say ourselves is clear and logical, and by encouraging our students, in the give-and-take of discussion, to order their thoughts logically, to give reasons for what they say, and to clarify what they mean when it is obscure.

There are three elements of clear and careful reasoning that we expect from our students all the time and often call for when we find them missing. The first is a clear grasp of the relevant facts, an ability to say precisely what the relevant facts are and to explain why they are relevant. The second is the ability to explain the meaning of key terms or concepts when they are vague or ambiguous. And the third is the ability to fill in the missing steps in an argument, explanation, or other piece of reasoning so that the conclusion can be seen actually to follow from the factual claims and premises on which it is said to rest. We all notice the lack of these features of clear reasoning when they are missing from something a student says or writes, and we frequently intervene to correct the situation. We don't always intervene, of course, because we usually have other things to do, but we could intervene more often, especially when we are discussing the moral issues involved in or related to our subject matter. We could make a particular point of doing so to strengthen our students' powers of clear and careful reasoning with regard to moral matters.

There are also two other ways that we could contribute to our students' growth in this respect. When we are discussing the moral aspects of our subject with our students, it is possible to carry these discussions a valuable step further by inquiring with our students whether the positions being examined involve any unstated presuppositions or any unstated commitments to particular values or views of human life.

A second way we can enhance this process is by applying a little extra reasoning in the other direction, towards the consequences of a particular point of view. Thus if we use, or one of our students uses, a particular value or principle to support a particular conclusion, it is often useful to inquire what other sorts of conclusions or consequences might follow if that value or principle were adopted as a guiding rule of conduct. If the conclusions or consequences that follow from it are inconsistent or somehow unacceptable, that suggests a need to revise or qualify the value or principle or else to explain what was originally intended more carefully. If the additional conclusions or consequences are harmonious and acceptable, this lends credence to the importance of the original value or principle and renders its significance and its content more precise.

The third aim I shall speak of is really a particular aspect of the first two, but it is something that is easily overlooked when we speak simply about strengthening our awareness of values and moral principles and about clear and careful reasoning regarding moral matters. This third aim of those who teach ethics concerns the impact on our choices of the social and institutional context within which our choices take place. Once again let me draw my example from the medical setting.

Medicine is not only a series of individual encounters on the part of individual practitioners and their patients; it is not simply a matter of the individual acts of judgment that are made in those encounters. Medicine is also an extremely complex social entity, with institutionalized values and priorities, institutionalized structures of authority and responsibility, accepted modes of training, accepted ways of reasoning, accepted patterns of action and protocol. These aspects of medicine deserve moral reflection and examination as surely as the individual choices of the individual practitioners and patients who are involved. But precisely because these features exist in groups of people, as social facts, precisely because they enter into individuals' perceptions and priorities and patterns of expectation so gradually and even unconsciously, these features of the medical setting are easily overlooked. We rarely examine them carefully and rarely compare the features of an institution as they exist with other possible alternatives.

It is a commonplace, for example, that the overwhelming emphasis in health care in our society is on repair, on the correction of an already existing malfunction or disease, rather than on prevention, on health as a positive goal, or on modes of adaptation to what cannot be repaired. This is a priority within medicine as an institution that obviously affects thousands of individual decisions day in and day out. Yet, although this is clearly putting one set of values before another within medicine as an institution, it is hardly ever subjected to careful examination, and alternative sets of priorities for the institution are hardly ever given a careful look.

Or consider the standard relationship between physician and patient. The physician is rightfully considered an expert on matters that the patient desires to know. But in the standard pattern the physician does not merely provide the patient with the needed information; the physician makes the decision for the patient. As patients, we habitually hand over decision-making power regarding our health to our physicians, and, of course, physicians are trained and constantly reinforced to assume it. The reason for this handing over of decision-making power is presumably the physician's expertise. But we have many relationships with experts in which decision-making is not handed over to the expert. Rather, the expert provides us, as the decision makers, with the needed information and with advice, and we make the decision.

Consider, for example, the relationship between your physician and a specialist who is consulted about your case. The specialist provides your physician with expert information and advice, but your physician does not hand over his or her decision-making power to the expert. Your physician takes the expert information and advice and makes his or her own decision on the basis of it. It would be possible for you to have this same relationship with your physician, taking his or her expert information and advice and making your own decision. But this is not the standard relationship between physician and patient by any means. There have been some challenges to this pattern over the last two decades, but the notion of "doctor's orders" is still alive and well.

My point right now is not to argue that an alternative relationship would be better, but rather to point out that important values are at stake in these widely accepted patterns and that alternative ways of doing things deserve our attention. Not just in medicine, obviously, but in every institution and social structure in which we function, there are accepted patterns and priorities that are easily overlooked but have powerful impact on our choices. As teachers of ethics we need to call our students' attention to this fact and stimulate them to reason both about what is and about the alternative priorities and patterns of action and authority and the like that might be. This, again, is something we can do for our students with a little careful reflection and a willingness to spend some time. This, I believe, is a third proper and attainable aim of those who teach ethics in the university.

The fourth aim concerns the manner in which a person actually proceeds in doing his or her deliberation, in coming to a judgment, and in making a choice, when faced with a situation in which important values or moral principles are at stake. I think we can do much to help our students through the particular choice situations that they will face by the manner in which we present ourselves and by the manner in which we engage them when we conduct discussions of the moral issues involved in or related to the subject matter we teach.

I am not talking here about the help we might give to students privately in the form of advice or counsel when they ask us for such help. Rather, I am talking about help we can give them by the way we handle the moral issues that come up in our ordinary teaching. If, in our discussions of moral issues, we encourage all of our students to participate and respond with respect to the contributions of every student who addresses the issue—if we work to bring out the insights implicit in each student's contribution, draw out those who speak, and help them explain themselves more clearly so that the other students will see the merits of what they are saying, we will communicate a number of important attitudes to our students. We will communicate, above all, respect for diverse points of view and a conviction that we can learn much that is important from people who may disagree with us. We will communicate that listening to others and being willing to learn from them does not mean that we have no values or principles of our own. We will communicate that, when faced with a difficult moral decision, we would do well to consult with others, to test out our knowledge of the facts, our awareness of the values and principles at stake in the situation, and our judgments and the choices we are considering against the insights and reflections of others.

These are valuable lessons. We may want also to stress the fact that in the last analysis each one must make his or her own final judgment and his or her own final choice. But by helping our students see the value of discussing their convictions and their reflections on the alternatives available to them with other persons, we will contribute much to their ability to form sound judgments and to make responsible choices in the future. And we, by our own example of treating every student's contribution with attention and respect, will give them valuable clues about how to go about this in practice, both how to listen to others and draw fruit from what they say, but also how to carry out the opposite role—how to be helpful to others who have choices to face, how to respond to their needs and concerns with understanding, and how to offer our own reflections on their situation, when we are asked, with modesty and sympathy.

We who teach ethics can contribute to our students' skills in all these ways and can help them over the long run to reach sound judgments and responsible choices in the concrete choice situations they face simply by the way we present ourselves and the way we engage them when we call their attention to moral issues and discuss these issues with them in our classes. Doing this well is the fourth aim of those who teach ethics in the university.

As I look back on the decisions I had to make last fall regarding my father's situation, I can see that my own years of being taught ethics, by my own teachers, by my reading and study, by my students, and by other special persons in my life, must have fulfilled these four aims fairly well in me. For I can see that I approached my decision with an awareness that there were a great many values and moral principles at stake, that they did not all line up on one side of the issue or the other, and that they therefore needed to be sorted out very clearly and the conclusions and consequences of each needed to be reasoned out very carefully. I was very much aware, perhaps because I have stressed it so much in my own classes, that there is an institutional bias in medicine against dealing with dying and with those who are dying, a bias in favor of technology, an assumption that laymen do not understand what is going on, and so on. Consequently I also knew that I would have to draw on my own resources to take account of other points of view. I was blessed with the wisdom and sympathy of my wife and some good friends, and with the support of other relatives and several good nurses, and I had been prepared by those who have taught me over the years to seek out such people's wisdom in time of need and to draw on their support.

In other words, the process that led to my judgment, which I am sure was sound, and my choice, which I am sure was responsible, did not last just a few days last fall. The process began a long time ago, and the list of people who contributed to my development, so I could make the decision when it arose, is extremely long.

And so I must tell you, in conclusion, that I am extremely optimistic that people can help each other grow in moral maturity. I am extremely optimistic that we as teachers—all of us in every division of the university—can help our students grow in their awareness of values and moral principles and in the moral powers that I have spoken of. We need to have a clear sense of the aims that are proper and realistic in this enterprise, and we need to approach our students with modesty and respect. If we do these things, I am confident that we will assist them in a very important kind of growth and that they, in years to come, will also find themselves most grateful.

Mr. Murdock: Thank you, Dr. Ozar. The five panelists here will now comment on the paper you have just heard. Our first panelist, Ms. Marilyn Birchfield, is an assistant professor in the Department of Maternal-Child Health of our Marcella Niehoff School of Nursing. Her master's degree is from the University of Chicago; her field of specialization is pediatrics; her primary interest is community health.

Dr. Thomas Donaldson, a member of the Philosophy Department, received his B.S. and Ph.D. from the University of Kansas. His publications in the area of ethics include coediting an anthology entitled *Ethical Issues in Business.* He has a forthcoming monograph entitled *Corporations and Morality.*

Dr. William Donnelly did his undergraduate work at Princeton University and received his M.D. from Loyola. He served his internship and residency at Cook County Hospital. He is today chief of the Hematology/Oncology Section of the Hines VA Hospital and professor of medicine in the Stritch School of Medicine. He has published in hematology, and his current interest is medical humanities.

Dr. Alan J. Fredian is the director of our Institute of Industrial Relations. His Ph.D. in industrial psychology is from the Illinois Institute of Technology. Prior to his coming to Loyola, Dr. Fredian was a management consultant and a corporate executive. He has published in the area of organizational development.

Mr. Joseph Lassner is a faculty member in our School of Social Work. He holds degrees from Brooklyn College and the University of Pennsylvania. Before he joined the Loyola faculty, he was engaged in social work practice and administration in New York, Massachusetts, and Connecticut. He has recently been involved in the revision of the Code of Ethics for Professional Social Workers and in the adjudication of charges of unethical practice.

Now, our first panelist, Ms. Birchfield.

Ms. Marilyn Birchfield: It is my role to continue with a discussion of nursing and the way in which we teach ethical behavior in the School of Nursing.

In this diverse group it would probably be useful first to examine briefly the role of nursing today. Nursing consists of the care of well and sick people in many different settings. It requires ability to care for patients in activities of living, to perform technical skills with safety, and to communicate with people of different ages in times of stress and crisis.

The many skills that the nurse acquires eventually are practiced in independent situations without supervision. Nurses may be held responsible for whether or not procedures are done, but there is little accountability for the *way* in which they are done. For instance, the nurse who contaminates a needle before giving an injection breaks sterile technique and must decide what to do. Will the nurse choose to change the needle or to give the injection with a contaminated needle? Obviously, in this situation, one solution is not as good as another, but the option to choose is available to the nurse. What makes him or her care about the patient and choose to protect the patient?

To understand how they make choices, students must have opportunities to examine what motivates their actions and how values will or should guide their behavior. They also need time to reflect on their values and to develop values that are congruent with their responsibilities. In the School of Nursing, meeting these goals is a part of human potential seminars and also a part of individual conferences with students.

An example of another nursing situation might be the nurse caring for a young child who is going to surgery. The nurse prepares the child physically and checks the chart to make sure that everything is in order, but has he or she taken the time to prepare the child for what is going to happen? In addition, does the nurse believe that preparing children for experiences in a way they understand helps to reduce fear and aids them in adapting to and recovering from illness?

Along this line I would like to share an experience I had recently with a student. The student was reluctant to begin the activities that are necessary to prepare a two-and-a-half-year-old psychologically for surgery on her eye. The student knew that this should be a part of the child's care, but she needed a "push" or encouragement to become involved with the child in this way. It is not the easiest thing to do and requires relating at the child's level. It meant teaching the child, as she eventually did, with a big stuffed animal and eye patches, and involving the child in what we call therapeutic play.

After observing the child's animated and active play, I was interested to hear the student's comment regarding the meaning of the experience to her. In a determined voice she said, "I believe—all of that play stuff seemed silly before, but now I believe." In her voice and in her manner, she identified for me the importance of having an opportunity to test out principles of nursing care that she had been taught but had not felt particularly comfortable with.

In nursing education, clinical or practice experience is a valued part of the curriculum. Students spend two to three days per week in clinical settings testing or validating what they have learned, as well as developing skills.

An exploration of ethical practice in nursing can also extend to include the policies that exist and guide the nursing care that is given in an institution where students and instructors practice. Educationally, if there is a difference between what the student is learning and what is actually seen practiced, the student may feel uncomfortable, even betrayed.

Students want to learn and believe in what works and what doesn't. It is critical to their feelings of security in their role. Many institutions are reexamining their policies today and need support as they revise practices that are no longer congruent with present beliefs.

For instance, the belief today in the right of the whole family to share in the birth experience has contributed to many changes in the maternity ward, where the welcome mats are out for both fathers and siblings, and where they are encouraged to become involved early with the new addition to their family.

Also, many of us in pediatrics believe in the young child's right to the continued presence and support of parents or parenting figures during illness and periods of stress. For many reasons, unfortunately, there are far too many children under the age of five who are still hospitalized without this support. The emotional trauma known to occur in these young children is well documented in studies and could almost be called a form of child abuse.

Obviously, we as teachers have a role in making the changes we believe in come true; we must engage in dialogue with our colleagues, the practitioners, demonstrating our concern and interest. In doing this, we can communicate to our students that we are not threatened or alienated by those who are different, that changes occur through planning and involving others, and that this does not mean that we have no values or principles of our own.

At one time the preparation of nurses was called "nurses' training," which was appropriate, as authoritarian people told us how we must do things. The development of many skills today still requires careful supervision, but it also requires an interactive process that increases a student's sense of responsibility and understanding of self and others.

Mr. Murdock: Thank you. Now Dr. Donaldson.

Dr. Thomas Donaldson: I liked Professor Ozar's paper very much. In fact, I liked it so well that I'd like to spend my short time guarding against a possible misinterpretation that it might be prone to.

Professor Ozar's emphasis on openness in the classroom reminded me of the Platonic dictum that virtue cannot be taught. But I'd like to begin by citing an informal paradox in Platonic thought. It is this: Plato thought virtue could not be taught, yet both he and his mentor, Socrates, spent the major part of their lives teaching virtue. Sometimes even Socrates' teaching of virtue landed him in trouble with the authorities. When he was accused by the Athenian citizenry of corrupting the minds of its young men, Socrates replied that he had merely taught them to place virtue before ambition. But the good citizens of Athens rejected his reply. They firmly believed their children should be educated in practical matters but saw little need for the study of abstract issues such as truth and virtue. In short, they wanted them to have a purely professional education, one that solely developed the arts of public speaking and negotiating public affairs.

But if Plato and Socrates taught virtue, why did they believe it could not be taught? I suggest the answer lies largely in the reasons presented in Professor Ozar's paper; for Plato knew that virtue could not be taught like rhetoric or horsemanship, where the principles are laid out for the students to pick up and memorize. Such a dogmatic approach is worse than nothing, for the more the student is forced to swallow what has not been chosen, the more likely he or she is to reject it. But if virtue cannot be taught, why teach it? Why was Plato, and why is Professor Ozar, a teacher of ethics? I hope to shed light on this, and if my hunch is right, Professor Ozar will not disagree at all with what I have to say.

Professor Ozar emphasizes how in teaching ethics openness is crucial. Without openness, ethics dissolves into lists of meaningless rules. But a distinction must be drawn between two concepts. These are "pedagogical openness" and "normative skepticism." By pedagogical openness is meant precisely the thing Professor Ozar was emphasizing: openness in the style of teaching and construction of materials that allows freedom of reflection. But pedagogical openness is not the same as, although it can be confused with, normative skepticism. Normative skepticism is a view or philosophical disposition that regards all ethical issues as relative. Like a smorgasbord, the field of ethics must be an exercise in which taste dominates. You like oysters; I like strawberries. We may pick what we like. Yet there is no reason to suppose my choices are better than yours. And it is important that the moral teacher not embody or give the appearance of embodying this view.

As Professor Ozar notes, if a student comes to an ethics professor, the professor should be reluctant to load him with advice. This is not only pedagogical openness; it is prudent behavior. The professor is not trained as a counselor, and often a student should be directed towards a professional: a priest or psychiatrist. Yet the professor risks the impression of normative skepticism if he or she appears to have *no* moral point of view. The professor's openness should not be mistaken for relativism. If the situation is of an acute sort, then advice should be given—sometimes with spirited firmness. For example, if a student in a business ethics class comes to the teacher distraught over having stolen $50,000 from the Harris Bank, then the teacher should advise that student to return the money.

If there were no distinction between pedagogical openness and normative skepticism, then one should structure one's course in professional ethics by randomly choosing ethical theories for the student to read. Why have the student read Aquinas, Plato, or John Stuart Mill? Why not blindfold oneself, spread all writing dealing with ethics on the floor, and randomly select the course material? If one ends up with a course focusing on the works of Machiavelli, Hitler, and Sade, then so what?

The reason for avoiding such a procedure is that we are all of us, even if we are not ethics professors, something more than normative skeptics. And if we happen to be professors of ethics, the student in class should not be encouraged to believe we are normative skeptics. Thus, to say that virtue can't be taught is not to say that there is not such a thing as virtue, or to deny that teachers of ethics can be important ingredients in the chemistry of the development of virtue. In the very dialogue in which Plato suggests that virtue cannot be taught, he goes ahead to compare the teaching of virtue with the teaching of geometry. Socrates is depicted in the famous scene with the slave boy. The slave boy does not know an important truth of geometry. Yet Socrates promises to teach him this truth, not by *telling* him but by *asking* him the right questions. Socrates is good to his word. He asks the slave boy a series of questions, and the boy himself comes, at first dimly but with increasing clarity, to discover the answer. Socrates thought the teaching of virtue was like this: the teacher must ask the right questions. If the teacher prods a student to reflect on the proper subjects, the student can then discover the truth. It's because Plato thought that there was such a thing as virtue that he devoted so much of his life to teaching it—or should I say asking about it?

Much the same is true of teaching in professional programs today. One fails as a teacher if one crams principles down the students' throats. Yet I personally am struck by the similarity of principles at the core of the great ethical theories. I happen to be a Christian and a Kantian. You may happen to be a

Moslem or a utilitarian. Yet whether we subscribe to teleology, deontology, Kantianism, Hinduism, Taoism, moral sense theory, intuitionism, or natural law theory, we will agree to the principle that it is good for people to possess a reverence for life and respect for the worth of others as persons. I will not preach even these general principles to my students in a class of ethics. I will certainly not grade them on whether they accept them; but I can hope they discover them. And I can promote the proper atmosphere and clear away some of the obstacles to aid in the process of discovering them. And this is the solution to the Platonic paradox: virtue cannot be taught, but it can be cordially invited to attend to its own development. Thank you.

Mr. Murdock: Thank you, Dr. Donaldson. We'll hear now from Dr. Donnelly.

Dr. William J. Donnelly: To begin with, I want to thank Dr. David Ozar for sharing with us the intensely personal and deeply moving story of his experience of his father's illness. My comments will be directed to this story and its value for me.

We can teach medical ethics in terms of principles or theories applicable to a broad range of problems. Alternatively, we can use case studies that illustrate and raise ethical issues and quandaries. For clinicians the case method has an immediate appeal. Physicians learn much of their craft from the personal study of individual patients and their problems. Additionally, such educational cornerstones as morning report, medical grand rounds, and clinicopathologic conferences teach by actively involving the conference participants in identifying, assessing, and solving medical problems of patients who are not their own.

Dr. Ozar's remarkable story is roughly analogous to the first portion of a physician's or medical student's case record: the history, or the patient's account of his or her symptoms and understanding of current and past illnesses. We can use it to illustrate ethical issues, just as we could use a case study that also included the physical and laboratory findings, diagnosis, and prognosis.

Let me comment on just one element of Dr. Ozar's account that can be used to illustrate a principle. Recall that the *doctor* raised the question of whether to attempt resuscitation in the event that the father's breathing or heart action stopped, but asked for the *son's* participation in the decision not to resuscitate. Why? Isn't this a medical decision? Was the patient's son consulted about the other treatment given, or considered and not given? The doctor's action illustrates the sometimes forgotten truth that the practice of medicine is value laden. When the patient's and the doctor's values are comfortably congruent, the values remain submerged and unexamined. In Dr. Ozar's account the doctor has made room for the patient's participation in a decision that involves personal values and preferences. In this instance, because of the father's inability to communicate, the son, as next of kin, was asked to decide for the patient. The doctor's actions illustrate that many nonmedical reasons are involved in decisions to limit treatment that might, for example, uselessly or painfully prolong the life of patients who are mortally and irreversibly ill. Further discussion of this case could logically lead to a basic principle: the right of competent patients for personal, religious, or philosophical reasons to decline not only cardiopulmonary resuscitation, but any medical or surgical treatment. I do not argue that the right to refuse treatment is an absolute right, but that's an issue for another day.

Dr. Ozar's story is important in another way. It differs from the medical history customarily elicited by the physician. Dr. Ozar's account, in fact, belongs to an increasingly important literary genre, the first-person account of illness written by an articulate patient or someone close to the patient, often a wife or husband. Examples are numerous. Norman Cousins' *Anatomy of an Illness* is a popular one. Lael Tucker Wertenbaker's *Death of a Man* is another. Recently, similar accounts have begun to appear in medical journals! These stories powerfully convey the reality of the *subjective* experience of sickness to physicians who have become increasingly preoccupied with *objective* data and disease entities. James Hillman reminds us that illness, even when the result of organic pathology, is "not only a clinical event. It is also, if not first and foremost, a psychological event whose physical aspects require a psychological examination."* The pain, dismay, and other feelings of sick human beings and their families are not always apparent to a doctor whose notion of the "real" is limited to what can be weighed, counted, or otherwise measured. Dramatic accounts such as Dr. Ozar's can help physicians get back in touch with the nonclinical dimensions of illness: what the illness means to the patient and his family. The result will certainly be a more humane and ethically sound practice of medicine.

Mr. Murdock: Thank you. Now Dr. Fredian.

Dr. Alan J. Fredian: Dr. Ozar and others illustrated some difficult decisions facing people in the health professions. I will discuss difficult decisions in organizations, especially business organizations.

First, by way of introduction, let me offer a short observation on a University of Pennsylvania study on managerial ethics. Two thousand people in ten countries were asked a hypothetical question concerning the ethics of executives in a drug company. The question was whether executives, if faced with the knowledge that a recently developed medication would be dangerous and could kill as well as cure, would take it off the market. All respondents said the decision would be to keep marketing the drug, even though 97 percent believed the decision to be irresponsible.

Why will people make decisions that they know are irresponsible? Are we trapped in a culture (a social or institutional complex) that inhibits our acting responsibly?

Let's look at that University of Pennsylvania survey question again. Suppose that your company was negotiating financing for the production of what appeared to be a very promising cancer vaccine and that, if you took that other dangerous medication off the market, you would lose your financing and the opportunity to develop the cancer cure in the immediate future. How would you decide? The decision is not an easy one. Many alternatives have to be weighed. The longer you spend on them, the less appealing quick decisions such as the following seem. "Take the drug off the market

*James Hillman, *Re-Visioning Psychology* (New York: Harper Colophon Books, 1975), p. 80.

now; we can't play God." "Turn the cancer cure over to someone else to make; it's for the good of humanity."

The process of thinking a question through and being aware of your values is a good one. That's why ethics courses are important: to make one more aware, to help think things through. A broad perspective is important to see *all* the consequences of our actions and decisions.

Some business people tell me that businesses exist only to make a profit. Frankly, I consider that an intellectual cop-out. These people have not been made aware of other values or have not thought through the total nature of a business enterprise. In my MBA classes years ago when someone talked this way, I had a standard challenge. "Name any company in this country and I'll guarantee that I'll increase profits over present management! Now this company may not be around next year, but they'll be more profitable this year." No one ever accepted the challenge. So! There *is* something beyond immediate profits. It's through the process of awareness and reasoning that we arrive at other values.

Now before we consider business people as those who need the most training in ethical principles and processes, we should be aware that most institutions put pressures on their members to act in constricted but acceptable ways in that culture. Robert F. Allen reports on the percentage of various groups and organizations that were identified by his respondents as encouraging poor ethics among members.

Businesses	79%
Government agencies	76
Political parties	74
High schools	65
Colleges/universities	62
Hospitals	41
Churches	36
Families	30

Only 10 percent felt organizations encouraged honesty.*
So it seems that many of us are victims rather than

*Robert F. Allen, "The Ik in the Office," *Organizational Dynamics* (Winter, 1980), pp. 27–41.

persecutors. Our salvation lies in knowing why we make decisions, what the influences on us are, and that we indeed can be free *if* we are true to ourselves.

For example, an Institute of Industrial Relations student who took Father McMahon's ethics class quit his job over a perceived ethical issue. He knew his values, saw he could not change the situation, and did not want to work for an organization that would force him to violate his principles.

In conclusion, it appears that for the good of society we need to look at "upstream" solutions that eliminate causes rather than effects. For our ethics courses, we have to be alert to the tendency to "blame the victim." Instead we should look for upstream approaches. Furthermore, we should continue to discover who we are, what is important to us, how it affects our behavior, and what are the consequences.

Mr. Murdock: Thank you. Our last panelist is Mr. Lassner.

Mr. Joseph Lassner: As the final panelist for both this section and the total symposium, I have a tremendous temptation at this point just to say "Me too." I will yield to that temptation with only a few comments to connect professional social work education to the material we have heard.

We in social work are particularly fortunate in that the short history of our development as a profession, from the early days of Jane Addams and Mary Richmond right here in Chicago, includes an identified value system as an integral and critically significant component. No student can come through the first course in practice methods in our school— no student can read any beginner's textbook in social work practice—without having read a list of those values at least a half dozen times and quite possibly committed many of them to memory. Let me enumerate a few of the more common and universal ones: a belief in the dignity and worth of each human being, a belief in the client's right to self-determination (our own Father Biestek* has written

*Father Biestek is Emeritus Professor of Social Work at Loyola University of Chicago.

extensively on this one), an acceptance of each individual's right to be different and an appreciation of that difference, and the interdependence of mankind.

So what? Now we have these high-flown statements, the students learn them and are even able to recite them back to us by rote; where do we go from there? Again a fortunate, but certainly not accidental circumstance. Our educational program has two sets of learning experiences operating concurrently: the field practice and the classroom courses. We like to say or think, in rather simple terms, that the student gains "knowledge" in the classroom and "skill" in field practice. Where does the third component of that eternal educational triangle of "knowledge, attitude, and skill," the "attitude" component, develop? We say, at least to ourselves as we struggle with this issue, that somewhere between the development of skill in field practice and knowledge in the classroom, we are doing something that helps socialize the student to our professional value system. Our belief that this system works is based on our old friend "practice wisdom," but little research can be found to support this belief with cold, hard facts.

Let us go back to social work history for another moment. In the mid-1950s, when the various splinter organizations in social work got together after years of discussion and developed our major professional organization, the National Association of Social Workers (NASW), one of the very first orders of business was the creation of a social work *Code of Ethics* and a standing Committee on Inquiry to adjudicate charges of violation of that code—a method of operationalizing and enforcing those high-flown values with a set of manageable guidelines. And that is what we do teach in the classroom. Let me list several of the fifteen ethical prescriptions for purposes of comparison to the more global values:

> I regard as my primary obligation the welfare of the individual or groups served which includes action for improving social conditions.
> I give precedence to my professional responsibility over my personal interest.

I respect the privacy of the people I serve.*

Earlier I said that I would like to say "Me too" to all that's been said before. May I particularly emphasize the fourth of Dr. Ozar's points, which I choose to label "modeling"—the behavior we demonstrate for our students, and the ways in which we relate to them? Some of the dilemmas faced by social work students in class discussion and field practice are of the nature referred to by Dr. Ozar—the need to choose between two "goods," the choosing between the rights of one party and the rights of another, both equally important and valid. These arise regularly when we deal with child care, family work, and divorce, among others. The method I find most satisfying in the classroom teaching of ethics and values for practice involves sharing my own dilemmas, concerns, and thinking processes as a practitioner and as a teacher and helping students to do the same.

Another form of modeling has to do with my own behavior as a teacher. If I really believe in the principle of confidentiality of client information, what am I telling my students when I publicly post on the bulletin board, or announce in class, exam scores or final grades? Am I not really modeling "Do as I say and not as I do"? Do I strengthen the principle of respect for individual differences and help the student to help the client to look at alternative ways of solving problems when my own classroom behavior indicates that my way is the *only right way*?

I would suggest that in the classroom we have an opportunity to be important moral, ethical, human models, struggling to make decisions and sharing that struggle with our students. Thank you.

References

Biestek, Felix P., S.J. *The Principle of Client Self-Determination in Social Casework*. Washington, D.C.: Catholic University of America Press, 1951.

Biestek, F. P., and Gehrig, Clyde. *Client Self-Determination in Social Work: A Fifty-Year History*. Chicago: Loyola University Press, 1978.

*National Association of Social Workers. *Code of Ethics*. Washington, D.C.: adopted October 1960; amended April 1967.

Mr. Murdock: Thank you, Joe. Time has flown and so I must abandon my five-minute response, but let me offer a quick perspective while the members of the audience formulate their questions. I thought it interesting that Dave talked about institutional values, that Tom talked about paradox, and that Alan mentioned that people in business sometimes make decisions in conflict with their own value structure. I think a paradox really needs to be addressed in that institutions in a sense are really a summation of the people within them; yet, as a Notre Dame study a few years ago on the electric power industry bore out, somehow or other administrators and employees manage to impute to institutions a value structure different from their own value structures. And so I think it is important to educate students not only to form their own value structure but also to see the significance that value structure has in connection with the value structure of the institutions within which they live and work, and to develop a certain amount of conviction in their own value structure so that they are willing to expose it and introduce it into the mélange of values within an institution out of which the institutional value structure comes.

The floor is now yours, and I'll accept questions or thirty-second speeches. Sometimes there's confusion between questions and speeches.

Dr. Harold Blumenthal: What about the tough decisions that nurses and doctors sometimes have to make—for example, when they make decisions that go against their peers?

Ms. Birchfield: I can make a brief comment because we did discuss this a little bit in our preliminary planning. In fact, in David's paper, originally some conflict was expressed about the role of nurses and doctors in decision making. I think that a nurse must be very careful, since the nurse knows all of the information that is involved in a case. And nurses must act on a basis of knowledge and responsibility, which would certainly involve some interaction with the physician to make sure they know what the physician is thinking about. I think sometimes we make very emotional decisions without really knowing what we're making a decision on. However, there can be very clear-cut situations where you see someone actually contaminate something, and you know that that is absolutely wrong and something should be done about it. But I've heard of situations where this is not done.

Dr. Donnelly: I think that Dr. Blumenthal raises an important point. He suggests that physicians often demonstrate more loyalty to colleagues than to patients. For example, physicians are often loath to blow the whistle on dangerously incompetent physicians. Fortunately, many medical societies now actively seek out incompetent or impaired physicians for counseling and rehabilitation.

Mr. Murdock: Responding to that, I think in teaching ethical behavior it is very important to get the point across that this behavior involves risks, that you cannot act in an ethical manner and be assured of being safe. In fact, Alan alluded to that. Ethical considerations led someone to quit his job; the student some day may face a similar decision prompted by ethical considerations. Joe?

Mr. Lassner: Somewhere in our two-year master's curriculum, every student is exposed again to the fact that our profession not only has a code of ethics but has attempted to put some teeth into that code. Some case examples are given of social workers challenging colleagues, charging them with unethical conduct, and learning some of the issues involved in how you make a charge, how you respond to it, and how your peers adjudicate it. In several places we have even done mock hearings of ethical charges around the choice between two goods or two perceptions of good. So some of that does go on.

Dr. Gerald Gutek: Let me preface my question by saying that I am for teaching ethics, a topic that has been developed during this symposium. There has not been, however, much talk here about learning. What is the direct relationship between teaching ethics and learning, and how is that evaluated?

Dr. Ozar: Let me do that in two pieces. First, I would think that the paper I gave could be rewritten to be a paper about learning ethics, so you could understand at least some of the elements of learning ethics in terms of the four aims I talked about. But there are other elements, too, in learning ethics, and these partly depend on the process that Tom Donaldson was talking about: the values taking root. You can put the seed in the ground; but you can't *make* it grow. You can't guarantee that part of the process. So this is all a risky business; it doesn't have certain outcomes. I don't know if that's much of an answer, but that's what I've got to say at the moment.

Secondly, as far as evaluation goes, a lot of the teaching of ethics that goes on in a university like ours, I think, and a lot that could go on that doesn't, is a small part of courses on other subjects. In courses that are formally courses in ethics, a lot of the people ask me, "Whatever do you do to evaluate? Are the students moral people by the end of the course? Do they get an A if they are, or what?" And what I say and what I tell my students is that I will grade on the formal subject matter of the course. What I'm concerned to see them demonstrating are the skills of *clear and careful reasoning* and, to some extent, an ability to articulate in clear ways some of the positions we have discussed. It would be part of the mistake I was talking about earlier and urging us to avoid if I were to say, "Well, if you aren't a good person, then you flunk the course or you get only a C." But you can evaluate the reasoning process pretty straightforwardly. So, while our evaluation is not phony, it does touch only one set of elements in the process of moral growth.

Father Robert Harvanek, S.J.: This afternoon Kevin Coley, one of the students, mentioned the time thirty years ago when the proportion of Jesuits to non-Jesuits here at Loyola was much higher than it is now. Though there is a sense in which that statement is certainly true, it does nevertheless bother me a little. In terms of affirming what a Jesuit would affirm and of living a life according to Jesuit ideals, I have encountered very few non-Jesuits at Loyola University. And I have heard no non-Jesuits in the two days of discussion we have had about ethics and values. Though the Society of Jesus is an all-male community, despite the evidence of the membership of one, perhaps two, women in its history, my remarks are intended to include all the members of the Loyola community.

Father Donald Hayes, S.J.: The whole point about an institution like Loyola and its contribution to the ethical discussion of some of the major problems of our day is important. So far we have been thinking in terms of forming students and ourselves ethically by teaching ethics. We have to raise some of the questions of values and ethics that only an institution can treat. Two examples: We do not have the resources of a Harvard, but certainly one issue that is going to be paramount in the coming years is the energy question and how this affects our educating students and ourselves for living in the coming decades. Another increasingly prevalent phenomenon is the failure of marriages and families in our society. It seems to me that, as an institution of higher learning, we have an obligation not only to teach ethics to individuals but also to make our contribution to some of the big ethical issues and value questions of our day—to pool our resources and make an institutional contribution to *help* solve some of these current human problems.

Mr. Murdock: I now call upon Father Thomas McMahon for a final summary.

Father McMahon: Father Small asked me to tie together this two-session symposium. I notice a parallel between last week's theory and this week's application. For example, last week we concluded with the statement that ethics is normative, or at least that there is a normative dimension to ethics. In the discussion this afternoon, the panelists presented views that showed that we are not always certain what the norms are; nonetheless, clearly they agree that some form of a decision-making process should be part of the ethical learning procedure. Secondly, last week the panelists stated that ethics is more than knowledge and more than a cognitive type of function. Today Dr. Ozar's paper stated that ethics involves awareness, reasoning, personal example, and respect for the attitudes of others. Once again, the panelists require ethics to go beyond knowledge and cognition. Thirdly, last week we talked about the need for a role model. Today the student panelists stressed the need for role models among teachers and administrators. The professional panelists also required teachers and professional persons to be role models. Fourthly, last week we concluded that there is a religious perspective to ethics, that we cannot really isolate ethics from the religious context. Today the students brought out the need not only for a religious context but also for a Jesuit presence and an Ignatian spirituality. Fifthly, last week we talked about the theoretical concept that structure is somehow related to ethics in a Christian university, perhaps in evolving from justice to charity. Today we discussed the role of structure in terms of professional societies, professional groups, and the codes of ethics they propose. However, there is some concern about the principles that are embodied in a code of ethics and their application to the concrete situation. Finally, I think we agree that some form of institutionalizing ethics is required in a Catholic, Jesuit, urban university.

Dr. James Barry: I just want to remind you that the president opened this symposium by asking you to think about ways in which we can further institutionalize this renewed emphasis on values and ethics. I invite you now to think about that further and to write either to him or to me about what steps you think we should take, what approaches we should have to make this renewed emphasis on values and ethics part of our institutional life.

My last point is merely a pronouncement, and that pronouncement is that the 1980 Loyola-Baumgarth Symposium was a great success. Thank you.